Teotihuacán
My Journey through the Serpent into Heaven on Earth

By Christine Judal

Teotihuacán:

My Journey through the Serpent into Heaven on Earth

Illustrations by Madison James

ISBN Paperback: 979-8-9991529-0-9

ISBN Digital Edition: 979-8-9991529-1-6

Acknowledgements

My sincerest debt and appreciation are to my teacher and mentor, don Miguel Ruiz, not only for my inspirations that are evident in every page of this book, but truly for guiding me into a life of deep joy and love. I am forever grateful for his guidance. I also want to acknowledge Betsy Chasse, who has been an invaluable partner in bringing my book to life. For years, I had considered writing about my inspiring journey. When I heard Betsy say that she would be working with a group of women who wanted to write their book, I knew this would be my opportunity to finally make it happen and bring my dream to life.

During the past year of writing, my husband, William Filler, has always been supportive and encouraging. I truly appreciate his presence and his love. Finally, for all my fellow apprentices and friends who have traveled with me, don Miguel, and his family, on our many journeys, weekends, and gatherings, I wish to share my sincere gratefulness for every smile, hug, and each moment of joy and amazement that we have shared along the way.

Praise for My Journey to Teotihuacán

This is a beautiful, magical story. It's both personal and universal, as it tells of Christine's spiritual journey while opening up possibilities for many others — even the young of this generation — to take similar journeys of their own.

I was moved by many descriptions of human interactions and transmissions of wisdom from don Miguel Ruiz and Teo itself. I found the book engaging and articulate, dealing with complicated concepts simply and clearly. It was a special treat for me, as I remembered many journeys I'd taken through Teo with my own students, recalling the wide-eyed wonder and gratitude of those rediscovering the truth of who they really are.

And what is that truth? Just as Christine so clearly says: that we are life, the force that moves our body and the planets in their orbits around the sun. That we are love, the very light found in the space between the stars. So, I couldn't agree more: in a world where nothing is true but we can believe in anything, let's believe in love!

– Brandt Morgan, Author of Vision Walk

Having spent many days and nights in the arms of Teotihuacán, Christine's book takes me back to the place that opened my heart and soul to life and unconditional love. After reading her book, if you haven't been, you'll want to see it for yourself.

– Betsy Chasse, Filmmaker, What The Bleep Do We Know?!

While reading the book, I began to relate the process that Christine describes with other Toltec teachings I had learned from HeatherAsh Amara and other Toltec teachers. This book helped me to understand the steps and their order in a new way that tied the other teachings together. I also appreciate how the story emphasizes the love she found within each day's adventures.

– Judith Olson Lee, Student of the Toltec Path

Teotihuacán
My Journey through the Serpent into Heaven on Earth

Table of Contents

Chapter VIII

My Walk in Conscious Radiance Toward the Angel of Death

Chapter IX

Welcoming New Friends to Teotihuacán

Chapter X

Revisiting Hell from a New Perspective

Chapter XI

From the Angel of Death to the Plaza of Fire

Chapter XII

Receiving A Blast from the Heart of Teotihuacán

Chapter XIII

The Final Ceremony

Chapter XIV

Homeward Bound

Chapter XV

Practice Into Action

Preface

An amazing opportunity came into my life during the spring and summer of 1994. I was invited to attend a series of monthly meetings with don Miguel Ruiz. These meetings were held in the living room of Siri Gian Singh and his family in Sacramento, California. Each of these meetings was an intimate gathering of friends and acquaintances, where don Miguel would always begin with a prayer to our Father/Mother God. He would then speak to us about the powerful Toltec spiritual teachings he received through his family heritage in Mexico. His message was always presented with deep respect and love toward each of us, helping us to achieve a greater understanding of ourselves and the world around us.

In addition to these monthly meetings with don Miguel, I began taking classes with two long-time students of don Miguel. These classes included "Mastery of Awareness" with Dorothy Lee and "Toltec Dreaming" with Larry Andrews. Each course included valuable teachings and experiential spiritual work that brought me a greater understanding of myself, especially regarding how my personal experiences and the many ways that the culture around me shaped my understanding of life.

In late autumn of that year, don Miguel presented an offer that, for me, would begin a life-changing adventure. He spoke very quietly, saying that "two beautiful angels" had come to him with a question. He explained that the "angels" were Siri Gian Singh's two young daughters, Maya and Guru Mantra. They had recently asked him if they could become his apprentices. Don Miguel told us that, because he could not say "no" to these angels, he realized that he could not say "no" to us, either.

It was an offer that sent chills down my spine and my arms. Every cell of my body seemed to resonate with "Yes!" This offer from don Miguel was not given lightly. We were instructed to think about it carefully. This apprenticeship would mean a serious commitment in the coming years, both to ourselves and to don Miguel. He did not want anyone to enter this commitment half-heartedly. Only those who truly wanted to devote time and resources toward our spiritual growth and development should agree to become his apprentice. We were given a couple of weeks to ponder our decision. For me, it seemed that my entire life had led me to this opportunity, and I wanted very much to experience this adventure. I took some time to reflect on the experiences of my life that had created a desire to welcome this spiritual quest, and decided to move forward with all my heart.

The apprentice ceremony, held as a weekend retreat in a peaceful country ranch in Ione, California, was deeply moving. Don Miguel helped us prepare and consecrate our "power sticks". We had been requested by don Miguel to carefully choose a stick from nature (about a foot in length), some red cloth, leather tie strips and feathers for this purpose. We understood that the "power" held in these sticks came only from the intent placed within them by ourselves and by don Miguel as he blessed each of them, one by one. He then held each one upward for a moment toward the heavenly light. Finally, he wrapped each stick in red cloth and handed it back to us so we could fasten the cloth around the stick with a leather tie. It was a sweet and heartfelt communal ceremony in which I felt that each person was equally loved and cared for by everyone there. I had never spent two full days with a group where everyone was held in community with pure joy, love, and respect.

As I drove homeward that Sunday afternoon, I hadn't gone far before I had to pull my car to the side of the road. I stopped driving and cried tears of joy when I suddenly grasped how deeply precious this experience had been and how much love had been shared by everyone! It was truly a dramatic contrast between my past experiences in every church I had ever attended. I had attended quite a few different Christian denominations in various communities up to that point. Even though Christ taught love, and Christian churches should reflect this love, it seemed to me that this weekend experience was much more loving than anything I had experienced before in any Christian church. That realization made all the difference for me. Over the coming years, I began to appreciate how don Miguel could always somehow "set the energy" to a very loving and respectful atmosphere in our gatherings. I am forever grateful for this amazing and magical gift to us, no matter who comes to our gatherings!

* * * * *

How did my early life prepare me to be ready to enter this new adventure? I want to begin my story by offering a glimpse of my long ago—a glimpse into a time when I was quite young and open to possibilities in life. In a way, you could say that I was both blessed and cursed to be coming of age in a time of great cultural and technological change. Perhaps, in the midst of this cultural and social transformation, I needed a deep spiritual anchor and loving connection that don Miguel's teachings offered in a way that my experiences in the churches had not.

In the 1960s, our culture began transforming much more rapidly than it had in the previous, calmer decade. As a young teenager, I sat mesmerized before our TV, hearing the voice of Neil Armstrong as he made that small step, yet giant leap, onto the Tranquility Base on the surface of the moon. Many things were changing then, and the pace of change has only increased since that time. My parents were born in early 20th-century Idaho, when transportation still involved walking or riding in a wagon or buggy. Electricity and sidewalks were almost non-existent where they lived. In contrast, my early life was much more modern. I was three years old when I went with my father to purchase our first TV. At this age, I had never seen a TV before, or even any motion picture. I was enthralled. While my father went to the front of the store to make the purchase, I tried to climb up onto the boxes stacked next to the TV on display to see if it had a door in the back where "the little people" could get inside!

As an older child, I had listened happily to the small, scratchy sound of rock and roll emanating from my first "transistor radio," which I sometimes hid under my pillow at night. I was deeply saddened one morning when I was home (playing) sick from my fifth-grade class. My TV program was suddenly and rudely interrupted by the news that President Kennedy was shot. That sad event seemed to usher in a time of increasing turmoil. Other horrors startled my young eyes, as five girls near my age were murdered by a bomb placed in their church. Soon afterwards, TV cameras brought the black and white images of beatings and fire hoses raining down upon marchers attempting to cross the Edmund Pettis Bridge into our living room.

The Civil Rights Movement eventually seemed to open many vistas of greater opportunity that resonated through the music and movement of my generation (and those a little older), demanding more openness and equality for minorities, women, and First Nation peoples. The vision and hopefulness of Martin Luther King's "I Have a Dream" seemed to tumble into fractures when assassinations, racial tensions, and violent protests appeared more frequently on our TV screens.

The Vietnam War began to challenge our view of "America Right or Wrong", contrasting with the relative unity and patriotism of the post WWII years. As a teenager, I marched in a war protest on the streets of downtown San Diego, past men in dark suits hiding in the bushes and upper-story windows with telephoto cameras, presumably capturing our faces for FBI files. I didn't know at the time that President Nixon had decided to wage a campaign against war protesters and blacks who were fighting for Civil Rights. The extent of this campaign was eventually confirmed a few decades later by John Erlichman, Nixon's domestic policy chief.

One memory of that time distinctly stands out. On a Sunday afternoon in late summer, I walked with my boyfriend through a Balboa Park parking lot on our way to a free concert in the "Bowl". We had attended several of these Sunday concerts that summer. On this day, I was barefoot and wearing a mini dress. Suddenly and unexpectedly, we came to what seemed within inches of more than 20 police with enormous black boots and Billy clubs beginning to form a line across the parking lot, blocking the entrance to the concert. I remember looking down at my bare feet so close to those big black boots! The policemen in riot gear weren't about to let us hear a note of the music that day. My fear at that moment was exacerbated by the recent killings of war protesters at Kent State University. I didn't know what was about to happen, but that day, we weren't planning to protest anything. We just wanted to hear some music in the park.

Coming face to face with the line of police in riot gear (or more truthfully, facing clubs and boots because the faces of the men appeared stern, impassive, and unresponsive) was certainly unexpected and shocking. In the moment, however, it simply meant that we turned and walked away. We decided to explore the trails in the park and enjoy the rest of our afternoon. With so much turbulence surrounding us in the culture, it wasn't too surprising to see how the authorities' fear of "revolution" by students and youth permeated our direct experience. For me and my friends, the revolution was more about transforming the culture from within to become more open and accepting. It was about finding ways to work together and build unity, not destruction. In many ways, the cultural turbulence of that time helped to open me to greater possibilities and value wider perspectives in life. It was an exciting time to be a teenager. Experiencing many shifting tides offered me the opportunity to be more open to new possibilities that life can bring.

It was during this time of cultural unrest that my father died. He was a sixty-five-year-old veteran of two world wars. Years before I was born, he had survived nearly four years in a Nagasaki, Japan, prisoner of war camp. From the nearby hills, he had witnessed the atomic bomb obliterate that city in one morning. He cried because he had essentially lived among them and didn't believe that women and children should suffer in this way for the cause of war.

In a way, my father's death was sudden and unexpected, but truthfully, he had been declining into alcoholism for years. We certainly didn't fully understand PTSD at that time, but I knew my mother had great empathy for what he had been through. I had been very close to him as a toddler, but these past few years had been difficult. I was alone with him at our home in Tahoe because my older brothers and sisters had all moved on. My mother was in Idaho, where her mother was dying. I called my mother that evening to tell her that Dad had fallen unconscious in the bathroom, and I couldn't help him get up. She took the next bus home overnight, only to find that he was already gone when she arrived in the morning. He had eventually gained consciousness enough during the night to make the few steps to his bedroom. A few hours after her return home, my mother received a call to say that her mother had died as well. She then decided to have my father's body brought to his home state of Idaho, where we had two funerals.

We returned home to Lake Tahoe a couple of weeks later. As soon as I stepped into the house, I could feel my father's presence there. It felt very heavy, like a weight pressing down upon me that my 13-year-old self was not happy to feel. For a couple of weeks, I tried over and over to ignore the feeling. At night, I could hear the wrought iron rings of our curtains moving along the rods from the pressure of his presence. I hadn't been exactly happy with him over the past few years because of his alcoholism and sometimes abusive behavior. I didn't think he should still be here at all. I remember thinking that maybe he was breaking some kind of universal rule to still be here. I could feel that he wanted to tell me something. I kept trying to ignore him over the next couple of weeks, hoping he would go away. I speculated that maybe he was simply afraid of the hell that I thought probably awaited him.

You see, when I was six years old, our preacher at the South Tahoe Southern Baptist Church had declared in his sermon that "Anyone who doesn't believe in Jesus will go to hell". I had gone right home that Sunday and asked my father if he believed in Jesus. My father replied, "No, I do think there's a God, but I don't think he wants us to sit around and sing praises all day". In my six-year-old mind, that settled his future. It was just a matter of fact (in my concrete developmental stage of understanding) that he would go to hell when he died.

Finally, one afternoon about two or three weeks after his funeral, I sat at the kitchen table doing homework. On this day, it seemed like he wouldn't leave me alone. So, I looked up and said, "Okay, tell me what you want, and then you have to go away forever." I was astonished to see something like a camera aperture begin to open, and I could see through the opening into where he was. What I saw was not the broken shell of an old man as I had last seen him, but instead I saw a tall, beautiful, golden oval. I could see only pure golden light without any distinctive human features, but it was clearly my father. Suddenly, some of that golden light seemed to flow through the aperture opening. It seemed to pour gently right into my heart. I remember thinking how sweet and lovely it was, like sparkling golden honey of pure grace. My thought was, "Oh, how my father has changed!" I wondered how this could have happened, and thought maybe God had changed him. I asked, "Did you see God?"

My father replied in a silent but perfect telepathic transmission, "No, it's not like that. But there are beings with me here who have helped me to see my life clearly and to see how I had not really been there for you these past few years. I just want to say that I love you and I'm sorry I couldn't be there in a better way for you. I've also been trying to get through to your mother, but she won't pay attention to me either. Please tell her that I love her." My father then told me that I should never be afraid of death. I asked him whether he was breaking some kind of universal rule to do this. He replied that there wasn't exactly such a rule, but the beings with him had begun to discourage him from this major effort to communicate because it wasn't working, and over the past weeks, it was becoming very difficult to sustain.

As an adult, I have come to understand how remarkable it was for a teenager to have such an emotional healing happen effortlessly in an instant! I remember feeling much lighter in the days and weeks after that, and life seemed easier and brighter. Of course, anyone who has lived with a sometimes-abusive alcoholic would understand how much easier life is when that person suddenly isn't there. At the time, I thought my feelings were mainly due to that. I didn't quite know what to think about my father's visit, or whether anyone would believe me if I told them about it. My mother was always very easy to live with, although she did ask me to sleep in her room for a while after my father died. I didn't know how to tell her about his visit. One day, I finally told her, "I think Dad loves you, and he's in a good place." She replied, "Yes, I think so, too."

As I was growing up, my parents took very different approaches to religion. While my father never attended church, my mother insisted that she, my sister, and I attend every Sunday. We went to the Methodist Church until we moved to Lake Tahoe when I was six. Since no Methodist church was in the area then, we went to the Southern Baptist church. Even at that age, I found the Baptist teachings harsh and thought that many of the members were hypocritical because they seemed judgmental and did not live Christ's teachings the way my mother did. A few years later, I often went with friends to their Pentecostal church, where I sometimes witnessed people speaking in tongues. I enjoyed the many songs we sang, but never felt at home there. The church communities just didn't seem very loving or welcoming, as if most of the adults were going through the motions more out of concern for being judged than for any other reason.

In high school, I came across a book by Carlos Castaneda. It was called "The Teachings Don Juan: A Yaqui Way of Knowledge". I was enthralled by the ways don Juan explained the world and especially the magical experiences that don Juan helped Carlos to perceive. I thought this way of understanding the world made a lot of sense, even though it was completely different from anything I had ever imagined. I wished then that I could have a teacher like don Juan! But that seemed impossible because, according to the book, don Juan would never appear to anyone unless he chose the student himself. I just didn't know how to find such a teacher.

Life has a way of bringing us to the ones who will teach us the lessons that serve our highest good. For me, having the opportunity to learn from the master Toltec teacher, don Miguel Ruiz, was the experience I both needed and desired. This experience has been a lifelong gift that I deeply treasure. Through these teachings, I have learned, through practice, how to see the world with the "eyes of love". Everything I perceive around me today reflects this love because I know that this love emanates from me, through the depths of my connection with our unknowable loving source. As don Miguel taught, the world around us is a wonderful mirror that faithfully reflects what we hold inside.

Introduction

As you read this book, I would like you to imagine that you are joining me on a journey to Teotihuacán, the home of the ancient Pyramids of the Sun and the Moon. I want you to feel the magic and the blessings of being supported in your steps toward a more expansive and joyful life. I would love for you to experience the offerings of the gifts left to us in stones by the ancient beings who created this sacred city. My journey with you is inspired by the vision of don Miguel Ruiz, who showed us how to journey on this path down The Avenue of the Dead toward our greatest realization of who we truly are and how we can explore our connection with our own spirituality.

Although, at many points during this journey, I will share my understanding of the teachings don Miguel presented to us, I want to emphasize that everything I share is from my own point of view. I have listened intently to the teachings over many years and absorbed them into my own understanding as faithfully as I am able. I will share my experience with the desire to impel you to find your own inspiration as you join me on this walk through the Feathered Serpent.

The Avenue of the Dead in Teotihuacán, according to Toltec tradition, forms the body of the two-headed Feathered Serpent, Quetzalcoatl. We begin our journey by entering through the pyramid-shaped Temple of Quetzalcoatl near the southern part of the site and emerge at the Pyramid of the Moon near the north end. This journey of several days provides many opportunities to dive deep into our conscious and unconscious beliefs. It is a challenging journey that requires an expansion of trust in our highest nature and a release of everything that does not serve the true living force within us.

The actual humans who built Teotihuacán are lost to antiquity. However, as we can see by the remnants of their work, we know that they were great spiritual visionaries, skilled builders, artists, astronomers, and farmers. Their story cannot be traced entirely through archeological or historical means. The city was already in ruins during pre-Columbian times when the Aztecs arrived and began to make use of the site for their own cultural activities and ceremonies. The name Teotihuacán comes from the Aztec Nahuatl language. It can be translated in many ways, including "the place where gods were created", "birthplace of the gods", or "place of those who have the road of the gods" (ref. New World Encyclopedia). Modern spiritual leaders, including don Miguel Ruiz Jr., have also called it "the place where humans recognize the divinity within themselves".

In the Aztec language of Nahuatl, the creators of this city were called "Toltec", which means artist or skilled craftsman. When they arrived, the Aztecs found many beautiful artworks, including mosaic and carved masks, jade figures, many obsidian blades and objects, clay vessels, and carved stone figures. Most of these items are no longer in Teotihuacán. They are displayed and stored in museums, primarily in Mexico City, as well as in other museums around the world. There is a small museum in Teotihuacán, adjacent to the Pyramid of the Sun, which houses a collection of artistic treasures, as well as a three-dimensional map of the site.

As we begin this journey, it is important to have gratitude for the ancient beings who built this sacred site as a guide to all those who will choose to walk down the Avenue of the Dead. In ancient times, Teotihuacán was a kind of university that drew people from South, Central, and North America. Native peoples from what is now British Columbia have, in recent years, honored and re-enacted their ancestral ceremonial walk from their homeland to Teotihuacán. Today, several archeological studies have unearthed evidence of pre-Columbian barrios surrounding the current site that have evidence of different cultures from various parts of the Americas. This indicates that people of different cultures and languages would live in separate barrios surrounding the site. Teotihuacán must have had a powerful attraction that would inspire people to leave their homes and spend months or years living there.

In the vision that don Miguel shared with us, Teotihuacán is a place that supports the relearning of our personal connection with our own spiritual nature. Teotihuacán is the place where humans awake and become the truth. And that truth "is nothing but unconditional love." Of course, it is not essential for us to visit Teotihuacán to learn this. Many ancient cultures have similar teachings. Most religions have roots in such teachings, although the evolution of religious dogma often obscures those roots. One thing that makes Teotihuacán particularly helpful is that it provides a kind of roadmap. When I first visited the site with don Miguel and his other apprentices, he revealed this map step by step over several days as we traveled down the Avenue of the Dead. Day by day, we experienced how each part of the site provided a greater understanding of how to release our limiting beliefs, which have created barriers that prevent us from realizing our connection with our own divine nature.

This walk down the Avenue of the Dead represents the journey through the body of the two-headed Feathered Serpent, Quetzalcoatl. As much as our faith, our intent, and our imagination allow, the serpent and the site itself assist us by helping to metabolize, or burn away, everything within us that does not support our True Spirit. If our work is done well, we ultimately emerge from our familiar prison of human limitations into the sweet acceptance of true personal freedom that embodies our divine nature.

When we make the choice to trust that force within ourselves that propels us to move toward our highest purpose, then going forward in our life, we can experience ourselves as a loving, creative, energetic force, filled with Life and Gratitude. Isn't this the way we were meant to experience our life? Isn't this what everyone truly wants? Do you think that it is possible to live your life in this way? What if our true spiritual quest is not about gaining skills or knowledge, but more importantly, about gaining trust in our inherent connection with the consciousness that permeates everything around and within us? Perhaps the walk down the Avenue of the Dead, and all the inner work that we do there, can help us achieve and strengthen that connection.

As we move forward in our Teotihuacán journey, we choose to become a modern Toltec warrior and an "Artist of the Spirit". In this journey (and forever afterwards), our art becomes our life, and our life becomes our art! Everything we think and do represents our artistic creations. Our life is our masterwork. I will sometimes use the term "warrior" because, as we will discover, there is a battle in which we must engage against the limiting assumptions and beliefs of our minds that have prevented us from living our lives in joy, freedom, and creative brilliance.

The Toltec warrior understands that our primary conflict is not with our true self, but with the false image of ourselves that we have learned to believe. This image grew from the knowledge that we have absorbed over a lifetime from the beliefs of our family and culture. This knowledge then dictates how we use our word with ourselves and with others. Our word is like a magic wand! By our word, especially the words we say to ourselves, everything we believe becomes reflected in the way we perceive ourselves and the world around us. Therefore, as a warrior, we must constantly stalk how we use our word. We must pay attention to the way our words make us feel and begin to choose love-based instead of fear-based thoughts and words each moment. In a way, we can say that we hold love in one hand and fear in the other. It is always our choice to decide which hand we will open. As a warrior, when we make a mistake, we simply choose again. To master our art, we must practice and learn to use our words carefully.

A wise person, William Arthur Ward, once said, "If you can dream it, you can become it." So, what I'm asking is for you, as you read through this book, to dream a little dream with me in Teotihuacán.

As don Miguel often reminds us, "Humans are always dreaming". What you think of as the "reality of your life" is actually your own personal dream.

19

No one else experiences the world exactly as you do. You interpret everything you perceive in your own unique way based on your unique experiences, beliefs, and assumptions. A friend who is with you in the same room may experience an event quite differently. All the events of your life and the way you experience them create your personal approach to dreaming. You have always been aware that you dream when you are asleep, but it's essential to understand that, in a similar way, you are dreaming when you are awake, as well.

In some ways, you can think of yourself as the master of your dream. But what have you mastered? Is it a joyful, loving dream most of the time? Or is your waking dream often filled with worry, stress, difficult situations, confusion, regrets, or unmet expectations? If you are always dreaming, why not create the most beautiful dream that you can imagine? Why not open your dreaming mind to the possibility of miracles? As Neale Donald Walsh reminds us, "Miracles rarely happen in the lives of those who don't believe in them." Our power journey in Teotihuacán offers the potential to help us transform our waking dreams into living our personal experience of Heaven on Earth, where every breath, touch, tree, and flower can be seen as "miracles", no matter where on Earth we live.

Imagination is essential if you choose to come along on this journey with me. Every human creation begins with imagination. It is the most powerful, creative force in our medicine bag. Even so, imagination usually gets the short shrift in our culture. In other words, it often gets unsympathetic dismissal and curt treatment. Without imagination, our daily tasks often seem like the "daily grind" rather than inspiring imaginative creativity. Imagination generally has less value than logic and reasoning when we are expected to have a "sensible" solution. We don't get much encouragement to use our imagination in our daily tasks.

In contrast, Albert Einstein wisely said, "Imagination is more important than knowledge. For knowledge is limited, whereas imagination embraces the entire world, stimulating progress, giving birth to evolution." He also added, "Logic will get you from A to B. Imagination will take you everywhere."

Our culture places more value on knowledge than on imagination. In truth, knowledge is always changing! Knowledge today is different from a century ago and very different from what it will be a century from now. Keeping an open mind is one of our most precious resources. As I often heard don Miguel exclaim to my fellow travelers, "You know too much!"

One of the biggest obstacles to our creative nature is the way we have been conditioned to believe and react. How can we expand our range of life possibilities so that we can make better use of our imagination and to make the most of our Teotihuacán journey. How can we shift the point of view from which we normally experience our life to a broader point of view that incorporates imagination and enables us to see beyond our usual field of vision? We know scientifically that there is a whole spectrum of light, of which our eyes can only see a portion. There is a whole spectrum of sound, of which our ears can only hear a limited portion. What if our conscious awareness has a similar limitation? What if we could expand that field to a greater conscious awareness?

Today, while cleaning my kitchen window, I had an interesting thought about the intersection between my current point of view, my field of vision, and my belief. As I cleaned, it would appear to me that the window was clean. I believed so and could see that it was clean with my own eyes. However, as soon as I moved my head to a slightly different point of view, I could see something that I couldn't see before that still needed to be cleaned. This kept happening every time I changed my point of view. My thought was, "Isn't that basically how we view the world according to our personal belief system? We think we see everything clearly from our own perspective, and it perfectly matches our beliefs." Maybe our friend sees from a slightly different point of view, and they see something different. Sometimes, we just can't understand why they see a mark or even something significant that we can't see at all. As the philosopher, Arthur Schopenhauer, once said, "Every man takes the limit of his own field of vision for the limits of the world."

When I coach a client or friend who has a problem they can't seem to resolve, I often ask them to look at it differently, but in a more playful way. For example, if they really like chocolate, I might ask, "How does this problem look like from the point of view of chocolate?" Or, if they like to cook, I ask," How does it look from your kitchen?" I might also ask, "How does it look from 30,000 feet?" Sometimes, just shifting our point of view, even in a fun way that makes a problem seem lighter, can be powerful and help us to realize a new solution that wouldn't have appeared to us before.

Point of view is immensely powerful and colors how we see the world in ways that we rarely comprehend because our "normal" point of view is such a habit that we usually and unconsciously take for granted. It just seems to us to be "the way things are". Changing our point of view can often feel uncomfortable, like visiting a foreign land. If we do happen to visit another country and can understand the language, it can be quite eye-opening to realize how differently, in many ways, people living there see the world.

In political science, there is a concept called the Overton Window. This is a model for understanding how societal ideas change over time and influence political decisions. For example,100 years ago in the U.S., a constitutional amendment was enacted to outlaw the manufacture, transportation, and sale of alcoholic beverages. Fast forward to today, and not only do people poke fun at the folly of that action, but now, many states have legalized the sale and use of marijuana, which had been publicly demonized in that era, even after alcohol prohibition had ended. Other examples of such shifts have come through the Civil Rights Movement, as well as changes in women's rights and interracial or gay marriage rights. Each of these examples describes cultural and political shifts in the Overton Window.

Perhaps you can see how this concept might apply to your own "acceptable window" of what you have decided is possible for you to believe and what concepts might lie outside of that window. Perhaps you can remember a time in your life when you held beliefs and strong opinions about things that you no longer find are within your "acceptable window" of belief. If that is true, your window has shifted.

From our modern understanding of physics, we know that the electromagnetic spectrum of light ranges from radio waves all the way to ultraviolet light. "Light carries information", instructs don Miguel. If it didn't, we couldn't have radio or television, but more importantly, our eyes wouldn't be able to convey a representation of the world around us to our brains. We don't see an object; we see the light reflected from that object. So essentially, the light relays information about the object to our eye. But perhaps light carries even more information than just the appearance of objects. Don Miguel once explained to me how each point in space intersects with an unlimited number of rays of light coming from all directions. Another point in space intersects with many different rays. Therefore, each point of view provides different information, and we humans create our beliefs based on how we have learned to process that information.

As don Miguel explained, the ancient builders of Teotihuacán placed their "silent knowledge" in the stones. Silent knowledge can often be challenging to understand with our cognitive mind. Perhaps it can best be understood through the intelligence and the language of our heart. This knowledge is a powerful ancestral gift that can only be accessed when the window of your heart is open to allow the light to enter and fill you with awe.

When we visited Teotihuacán, don Miguel would sometimes ask us to remove our sunglasses so that the surrounding light and its pure information could enter our eyes without being filtered. I wonder how this pure light has helped to ignite a powerful transformation within me and my fellow travelers who journey down the pathway of the Feathered Serpent.

Before we begin, I want to share a dream I had years ago. In my dream, I am at home with don Miguel in my kitchen. As we talk, he notices a cheap, red plastic bowl on my table. He tells me, "I want you to look into this bowl and see the entire universe." I am intrigued as I look deeply into the bowl. I begin to see the appearance of the molecules beyond the surface of the plastic. These molecules start to dissolve into the entire history of humanity, speeding back through time. Soon, I begin to see Earth's history backwards through geological time. After that, I see the universe extending back in time through the cosmos.

After I see into the vastness of infinite space, the whole scene begins going forward in time…back through the cosmos, the formation of Earth, the evolution of plants and animals, and into the whole of human history. Finally, I can again see the molecular structure of the plastic bowl and then the bowl itself. I look up into the face of don Miguel and delightedly say, "I did it, Miguel! That was amazing!" I look down at the simple bowl and wonder how that was possible.

Then, don Miguel gave me an assignment: "Now, I want you to write down exactly what you did so that your students can understand how to do it."

Later that evening, still in my dream, I began to write down my instructions for how to see the universe in the bowl. I write a full description of exactly how I saw the whole universe. I think to myself, "This is good. But I wonder if my students would be able to understand." So, I decide to shift my point of perception to match my students' point of view. When I do that, the whole thing I just wrote makes no sense at all. I see that what I wrote might as well just be gibberish!

I tear up my paper and begin again. But the same result happens again and again. I begin to feel anxious and upset. I think, "How can I tell don Miguel that I can't do this assignment?" These concerns awaken me from the dream.

Still feeling a bit disheartened the next morning, I shared the dream with my friend Oliver, who was visiting from Germany. He exclaimed, "But don't you see? It's all about shifting the point of view or the perspective from which you are perceiving. That's exactly what you were doing in the dream!" I was very relieved and grateful for Oliver's ability to see the whole point of my dream. We laughed together.

As don Miguel has shared, "Wherever knowledge comes from, it is only real from one point of perception. Once you shift the perception, it is no longer real." Shifting perspective is something that humans do often, although most of us do it without awareness. For example, there may have been mornings in your life when you woke up, and everything seemed to flow easily. Perhaps you found every stoplight green as you drove to work or school. Your tasks seemed more effortless, and your co-workers were more friendly and helpful. Another morning, nothing in your world seemed to go right. That's an example of a shift in perspective! A fundamental rule of life is the beautiful quote from Wayne Dyer: "When you change the way you look at things, the things you look at change."

When you join me on this journey of heart and adventure, I ask that you honor your imagination, perhaps shift your point of view somewhat, and keep your "acceptable window" of possibilities open to the light of Teotihuacán. Remember to be aware that humans are constantly dreaming, have gratitude for our human ancestors who created Teotihuacán, and choose to experience this journey as an Artist of the Spirit! If you can join me in this way, you may be as surprised and filled with wonder as I was on my first spiritual journey there.

As I share my experience of this journey, some of my experiences may seem unbelievable to you when you first read them. This memoir of my journey shares my experiences as I have lived them firsthand. It is shared with all my love in the best way I can share it. Even if you think I may seem somewhat delusional at times, that's ok. I know that I am always dreaming, as we all are. If my experience of my life is a dream created by my mind, my choice is to make it a beautiful one. You can make your own choice. It's not important to me whether you believe me, but simply that I offer you something to ponder as you travel your own path through life.

Now, my dear friends, if you are ready and open to shifting your perspective a bit, I would be very grateful to have you join me on this transformative journey in Teotihuacán. I invite you to walk with me through the body of the Feathered Serpent and, in this pilgrimage, find some treasures that have always been held within the truth of who we are as Spirit and Light. I welcome your companionship.

"Living in a world of Miracles

Is living the life of spirit on this earth.

It's being in the world but not of it.

When you become more of your true self,

You begin to live the miracle.

It's simple, because you are that miracle."

- Michael J. Tamura

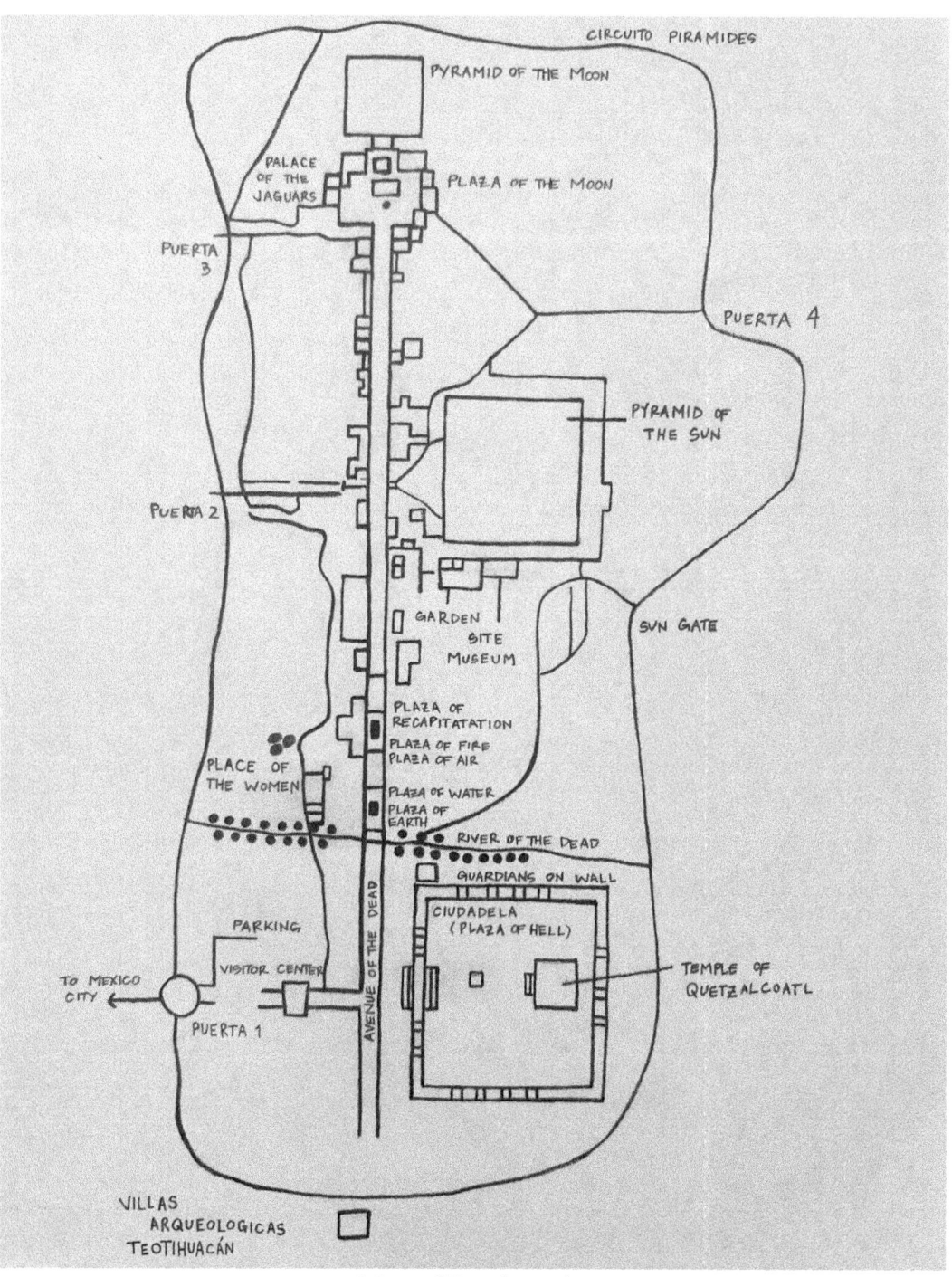

Map of Teotihuacán

28

Chapter I
The Journey Begins

We begin our journey early one January morning in 1997. I awake about four a.m. to prepare for my first flight to Mexico City. It is a cold, foggy morning, as often occurs in the Central Valley of California, where dense fog in winter sometimes lasts for weeks on end. I have spent the night with my dear friend Betty, who will accompany me on the journey. Judy, another friend and apprentice of don Miguel, will also be traveling with us.

It is about 5 am when Rachael and Judy arrive to pick us up for the ride to the airport. I am amazed at Rachael's calmness as she negotiates the back roads through Sacramento toward the airport. Not only is it still very dark, but the fog is so thick that I can barely see the road beyond a dozen feet in front of her car through the early morning darkness. I wonder how an airplane could possibly get off the ground with such poor visibility. At the very least, I expect that there could be a potential delay in our flight to allow the fog to lift.

When we arrive at the airport, Betty, Judy, and I are pleasantly surprised to find that the flight is scheduled to leave on time. The first leg of our flight will be to Phoenix, where we will need to change planes for the flight to

Mexico City. We check our bags and head upstairs toward our gate. As we walk toward the escalators, I find it amusing to hear the cavernous entry hall filled with the crowing of roosters! There are about a dozen crates filled with some magnificent birds stacked in the center of the hall. I wonder whether they are headed to a rooster competition, but that seems like an odd event for early January since county fairs don't usually happen this time of year.

The three of us locate our gate and get in line. There are just a couple of other passengers waiting ahead of us for check-in, but no airline personnel are yet at the podium. The sign above the podium indicates that our flight is still scheduled to depart on time, although I can see through the large windows in the waiting areas that the fog still looks very dense.

It is a while before someone comes to stand behind the podium, but they immediately get on the phone, so our line doesn't move forward. Eventually, I notice that our flight status has changed to "Delayed". The first passenger from our line to be helped seems to take a very long time with the check-in staff. He is probably trying to reschedule his itinerary, but it doesn't seem promising. As we wait, I overhear the woman behind us frantically calling every airline and other airports throughout California, hoping she might be able to get another flight to Arizona, but she doesn't seem to be having any success. We have been waiting in line for about 45 minutes when Judy turns toward me to say, "If we can't go today, I'm not going."

Judy is a second-grade teacher, and she is concerned about being away from her class for too long. It seems to me that it would be such a shame for her to miss this opportunity completely after all we have done to prepare for the trip. I decide to check in with my intuition about whether we are actually going to fly today or not. My intuitive response is a definite "Yes," even though I'm not sure how we can possibly fly in this weather. I then intuitively ask whether Judy will definitely also be going. The response I get is that she is definitely coming also! I can feel in my bones that there is no way we are not going, and Judy is going, too.

How could that possibly happen? I am pretty sure from my previous experience that the fog outside isn't going to lift today, and from the frustration

I hear from the woman behind us, other airports in different parts of California don't seem possible either. So now, I decide to check in "energetically" with don Miguel. I think if anyone can help us get to Teotihuacán, he can! I silently ask, "Miguel, how are we going to get to you in Teotihuacán, with the fog so thick and no planes able to depart? The airport here is completely shut down due to the dense fog."

It isn't more than 30 seconds after I energetically check in with don Miguel that the woman behind us asks, "If I rent a car, would you three like to drive with me to Reno, where we can get a new flight? I'm very anxious to get to my daughter's wedding. I've tried every airport in California, all the way down to LA, but all the airports are shut down today."

What a fantastic idea! Of course, we will go to Reno with you. Reno's in the high desert, so there won't be any fog there. First, we need to get our bags back and make sure the roads are open over the Sierra. Even the busy Interstate 80 in the Sierra can sometimes be closed this time of year if a recent snowstorm has made road conditions unsafe. However, everything soon comes together, and we head out of the dense valley fog and into the sunshine of the beautiful snow-covered Sierra.

It is a gorgeous drive over the mountains. I feel such relief and gratitude for the generosity of our rescuer and marvel at how soon after energetically contacting don Miguel that everything has changed in such a beautiful and dramatic way. I can't help but feel that somehow don Miguel has worked a little magic for us!

In Reno, we are able to book another flight that leaves later tonight, not to Phoenix but to Las Vegas instead. In Las Vegas, we will then have a two-hour wait before our 2 am flight to Mexico City. Our new flight won't depart until the evening, so we have time to enjoy an afternoon movie and an early dinner. I am relieved to know that Betty has a way to contact someone at our hotel in Teotihuacán to let them know when we will arrive in Mexico City after our unexpected delay.

Our flight from Reno goes well without any further delay, but I'm quite exhausted by the time we arrive in Las Vegas. I'm surprised how noisy and full of cigarette smoke the airport terminal is. Despite my exhaustion, it is hard to get any rest with all the commotion and slot machine bells going off. Eventually, it is time to board our flight, and I am glad to finally get a little rest.

It is early morning when we arrive in Mexico City. Our customs checks go very smoothly. When the frosted opaque doors finally open for us to exit the customs area, we soon spot our driver, Federico, standing in the waiting crowd, holding up a sign that says "don Miguel". Even though I don't know him, as soon as I see his sign, I know right away that this man has come for us. I feel very relieved to see him because I wasn't at all sure what to expect once we arrived in Mexico City. Federico shows us where to change our money and then leads us through the airport to where he has parked his car in the airport garage.

Soon, we are driving through the morning rush hour in Mexico City. I am impressed by how Federico can calmly negotiate our way through the hodgepodge of cars, trucks, pedestrians, and buses. The ride is very interesting and different from any morning drive I have ever experienced in a California city. Federico uses his horn courteously and often to help clear the way for his car to move forward. At one point, I notice a worker pushing a full wheelbarrow appear right before us in the middle of a three-lane traffic boulevard. Federico narrowly misses hitting the poor man. The worker suddenly realizes his error and runs back toward the curb, abandoning his wheelbarrow, which is soon demolished by the oncoming traffic. I glance over at Federico, but he drives on, calmly focused on the traffic.

We leave the city and drove northeast through the countryside. There are several toll roads along the way. The drive through the open country in the morning sunshine is a beautiful contrast to the bustling city. There are many farms and roadside shops. The air is warm and full of new scents. We pass fragrant fields along the roadway, and sometimes, the less fragrant scents of a pig sty drift through the open windows. The countryside reveals a simpler composition of life. It seems to me that everything is closer here, with less separation between humans and the sources of their livelihood and sustenance. It is quite different than what I usually experience at home in California, but very sweet in its own way.

After an hour or so, Federico turns off the highway and negotiates a right turn off the roundabout onto the Circuito Piramides. I get my first glimpse of the sacred city. From here, I can see the top of the Pyramid of the Sun gleaming in the morning light. It takes my breath away for a moment. A few minutes later, we begin unloading our bags at our hotel, the Villas Arqueológicas Teotihuacán.

After checking in, I notice that our friends (don Miguel had only allowed apprentices to attend this trip) are just finishing breakfast in the hotel restaurant. When I greet don Miguel, he gives me a big hug and says, "You are here. Now we can begin!"

"Humans perceive truth, but the way we justify

And explain what we perceive is not truth;

It is a story.

I call this story a dream.

The human mind mixes perception.

Imagination and emotion

To create a whole dream."

- don Miguel Ruiz

Plaza of Hell

Chapter II
Entering Teotihuacán and the Plaza of Hell

After a quick breakfast, we locate our rooms and head down to the hotel's biblioteca, our group meeting area. The room is already filled with our friends and fellow apprentices. As always, when we gather with don Miguel, there is a joyful anticipation in the air. I find an open place to sit on the floor near don Miguel and Gini Gentry, who has organized and planned the trip. Gini gives us the rundown on what we should keep in mind during our stay and tells us that if we need anything or want to complain about something, she has appointed one of our fellow apprentices to be the receiver of complaints. We should go to him for anything first—to say our room is too hot (it's January) or whatever else isn't right—even if he is unable to do anything about it. We laugh, knowing this isn't the first time Gini has organized a trip like this. She knows that a group like ours can potentially come up with all sorts of crazy things they think need attention. Going first to a friend who isn't in charge gives us a good reason to think twice before asking for help, and it certainly works better for everyone that way.

Now, as is his custom, don Miguel begins with a prayer to Father and Mother God, offering our gratitude for bringing us together here in this sacred home of our ancestors. He speaks to us of the changing of the light, as the sun is moving along the Toltec timeline from the Fifth Sun into a time of transition to the Sixth Sun. He explains that this is part of a greater Toltec understanding of time and that, as the light from the sun changes, everything on Earth will be undergoing a transformation. During the time of the Sixth Sun, there will be significant changes in human culture, as well as many other changes happening around the Earth. He says this transformation will be a gradual change, probably lasting decades. He hinted that this transformation was historically anticipated to happen approximately around the year 2012, coinciding with the end of the current Aztec calendar. When don Miguel came to Teotihuacán in 1992, he witnessed that this change in the light was already beginning, although it will continue to shift gradually. He tells us that we are living in a wonderful time. We are part of the transformation of humans. It takes time to complete the transformation. If we have resistance, it will take longer, but it will still happen.

The Toltecs estimated that each Sun lasts about 5200 years. In many ways, the Fifth Sun has primarily been a time of male-dominated outward action, in human terms. In contrast, the Toltecs believe the Sixth Sun will be a time of inward focus and creativity, the birth of a new consciousness with higher awareness of our collective well-being. As I ponder these things, I realize that we have arrived at this historical site during a very significant time of change. I feel that coming to Teotihuacán during this time of transformation is a very special opportunity for me to embrace transformation in my own life, and I'm excited to see what is in store for the coming days.

We are asked to prepare ourselves in reverence for our first day in Teotihuacán. It is important that we bring water, wear hats, and that we walk in silence to the site entrance at Puerta 1. We must remember that we are here for an important reason. We must not engage with others, especially the many vendors around the site, who will try to distract us by offering trinkets for sale. There will be time for shopping later. For now, we must focus on our inner purpose.

As we begin walking, I take in the sights and smells of the warm, late morning in this semi-arid region of Mexico. A few small cars and taxis pass us as we walk along the side of the road. We are going in the opposite direction from the direction we traveled when Federico first brought us to the hotel earlier that morning. I am awed by a distant vision over my right shoulder of the Pyramid of the Sun, gleaming a pale gold reflection in the morning sun.

After walking for about twenty minutes, we reach the roundabout near the parking lot entrance. Already, several cars partially fill the lot since it's a Saturday and just an hour from Mexico City. The day is already beginning to warm. I'm glad to reach the row of pepper trees offering dappled shade after crossing the warm, dusty parking lot. We briefly wait near the gate as our tickets are purchased, then enter the walkway lined by small shops offering trinkets, clothing, hats, and other items to buy. After passing through the visitor's center, we try to avoid looking any wandering vendors in the eye so they don't try to tempt us with their wares. They wave pretty necklaces and carved obsidian figures toward us, exclaiming, "Only one dolla for you". I can see that the items being waved must be worth more than one dollar, so I think the vendors are simply trying to entice us to engage with them for a sale--probably for a different item.

We cross an open expanse toward the steps of the Ciudadela. Upon reaching the landing at the top of the steps, I find myself standing beside don Miguel, on the precipice of my first Teotihuacán adventure. I feel a deep sense of growing trust, yet I'm apprehensive about what is yet to come. His kind, dark eyes sparkle with a deep inner joy that radiates warmth and confidence in the simplicity of life. He is surrounded by an aura that draws me into its warmth yet challenges me to the depths of my soul. He has invited us here on the threshold of a new adventure that will challenge the very essence of everything I have known, everything I have believed, and everything I have dreamed.

Our group expectantly stands together as friends and companions on the top step of a stone wall that surrounds a vast plaza. Don Miguel explains that this plaza represents a replica of the human mind. In essence, it represents the mind of a human who is immersed in the dreams and beliefs of human culture–beliefs based primarily on fear–that prevent humans from realizing the truth of who they truly are as divine beings. He calls this area the "Plaza of Hell". He says that this plaza holds both a fortress and a temple. As I take in the view from our place on the top step of the wall, I can see a large open plaza surrounded by something like ramparts. Every structure I see is made of stone blocks, mostly fastened together with mortar that is often punctuated with small black or reddish lava stones. The plaza appears to me as an ancient place of ceremony where people once gathered for rituals long lost to the passage of human memory.

The warmth of the dusty open plaza rises into the air surrounding us. Many people, including tourists, families, vendors selling trinkets, and groups with local guides, are walking through the plaza, many seemingly heading toward the more distant recesses of the plaza. I feel a curiosity to see what is drawing them there, but I am held in place by a fascination within what don Miguel is sharing. The clarity of his vision seems to overshadow the warmth of the day, the dust in the air, and whatever the humans around us are busy doing in this moment.

Don Miguel asks us to look around at the high walls surrounding the large plaza. In order to understand how this place represents a replica of the human mind, he explains that the human mind is designed to dream. Humans create dreams both while we sleep and when we are awake. We never stop dreaming. The dreams we create while our body is awake have many shared beliefs that enable us to communicate with others and to share our experiences. Humans naturally look to one another for reassurance that our waking dreams have shared understandings. In this way, together, we verify the reality of our experience.

Don Miguel has called this shared "reality" that is based on our beliefs "The Dream of the Planet". Because humans use our energy to maintain these beliefs, we can say that it is a living being. As a single human, we did not create this dream. It existed before we were born. In order to thrive in our culture, we adopted these beliefs as children without question. In essence, we personally agreed to those beliefs held by our family and culture. This is how the outside dream (The Dream of the Planet) became our inside personal dream—our own beliefs and perceptions.

As don Miguel explains, this plaza (also known as the Citadel or, in Spanish, Ciudadela) is well fortified. It is surrounded by tall stone walls, representing how humans defend our beliefs and identify so much with them that we can't imagine who we could be without them. He points out the elevated stone structures in sets of three or four that appear near the center of each wall on each side of the plaza. They are a significant part of the wall because they represent the guardians of the dream. As long as we humans continue to validate our waking experience with one another, selecting our beliefs from those that match others around us, we are not challenged by the guardians. They hold us within the walls in what we recognize as relative safety and harmony. Here, we engage in a shared experience, a community, a culture, and a "solid" structure upon which to live out our lives. Our knowledge and our beliefs are our own creations, which form the foundation of our personal dream. We allow this dream to control us even when it's not exactly true.

In the center of the plaza is an elevated, rectangular platform, a mesa, with steps on the left and the side facing us. Don Miguel calls this platform the "Island of Security". Beyond this platform, I notice another set of higher and steeper steps. But first, don Miguel calls our attention to the open space around the center platform. He refers to this area as "The Sea of Possibilities" for the human dream. He says that this "Sea of Possibilities" provides us with potential beliefs through which we create our personal belief structure. This belief structure determines how we experience our "reality". For each human, our set of beliefs become our personal Island of Security. Many of the beliefs an individual human holds are passed down by family, community, and culture. Other beliefs we may choose for ourselves, but only from the surrounding Sea of Possibilities. Mostly, we aren't aware that we have chosen or agreed to our beliefs at all. They are such a part of ourselves, ingrained into how we experience life, that they are like the air that we breathe or the glass in a windowpane. We normally don't see them at all.

As we step down into the dusty plaza, we are given our first assignment. It will be a challenging task that requires a willingness to go deep into how our life journey has been up to this point. We are here to stalk our dream, to discover how our beliefs have structured the way we dream, which then determines how we experience our life. We must each wander alone through the plaza yard, into the "Sea of Possibilities," searching to see the ways our lives have provided us with experiences from which we created beliefs that built the structure of our "personal reality."

We are not here to see ourselves as victim or judge, but to recover our integrity. We must look back at our life to see how our actions were dictated by our knowledge and belief system and how all of that was dictated by the outside dream. All humans do this. We must realize how all those opinions originally came from outside us. That's not free will! We must see our personal dream and make a choice to no longer be slaves of our old belief system.

For this task, each of us must ask ourselves, "What do I believe?" "What things in my life make me feel safe?" "What are the things in my life that help me to have security each day?" "What do I value?" The answer to these questions defines the things for which we must find and gather simple representative objects, like pebbles, flowers, or other small items, as we wander through the sea of possible beliefs.

When we have completed this task, which may take a couple of hours or more, we will bring our collected objects to the mesa structure in the center of the plaza. For each of us, this mesa represents our personal "Island of Security" that is built by our belief structures that help us feel safe. They create the "solid ground" upon which we walk through our life. Our particular chosen beliefs are only a subset of all the potential beliefs that exist in the Sea of Possibilities that surrounds the safe, solid island. When we finally arrive on this mesa, don Miguel will join us once again.

After this introduction, I begin to wander through this "Sea of Possibilities", trying to think of all the things in my life that contribute to my feeling of safety or security. At first, my mind goes to some of the more material things, like my car, home, family, job, and money. I find pebbles to represent each of these things. It's a little more challenging to think about beliefs that make me feel safe. I think about my reputation, intelligence, skills, and the way that I have learned to take care of myself and my family. I examine how I have come to see myself as competent or not competent. I remember don Miguel saying something to the effect of how we can also find security in our suffering and our shortcomings. We may say to ourselves, "That's just the way I am." So, I have an idea of who I am and act accordingly. I now wonder, "What if that is just a mask I've been wearing?" I find another pebble to represent my masks. By now, I have collected a pocketful of pebbles and a flower, but I can't help feeling that I have only scratched the surface of this task. I resolve to keep examining more beliefs over the coming weeks and months.

After completing our task as well as we can, we gather on the center platform, our Island of Security, where don Miguel asks us to contemplate each of the objects we have collected, remembering how that particular belief has served us. We are to have gratitude for that belief, for the meaning that it has brought to our life, and for all the ways that it has made us feel safe. However, we are also asked to recognize that anything we have used to feel safe is just a part of our personal dream. It isn't something that we were born with. Instead, it's something to which we have become attached. We begin an important step toward personal freedom by acknowledging and releasing these attachments.

Our task now is to bury these objects in the soil of the platform. We don't have to dig a deep hole; we just need to cover the objects with a little loose soil. This act represents our willingness to let go of old beliefs and attachments that no longer serve us on our path to freedom. As I cover my set of stones and a small flower, I feel a sweet sense of both sorrow and gratitude for these things that have meant so much in my life. But it also feels good to release my attachments to these beliefs. I feel a sense of lightness, as if I am stepping into a greater acknowledgment of my true being and Spirit!

"When you come to the edge

Of all the light you have

And must take a step

Into the darkness of the unknown

Believe that one of two things will happen.

Either there will be something

Solid for you to stand on

Or you will be taught

How to fly."

\- Patrick Oberton

The Temple of Quetzalcoatl

Chapter III
The Temple of Quetzalcoatl

After this powerful ceremony of release, we descend back into the Sea of Possibilities. We are asked to gather with don Miguel at the base of the higher set of steps toward the back of the open plaza. From where I stand at the base of the steps, I can't quite see what is at the top—it's quite high. We are encouraged to close our eyes and imagine a very dark night with no moon visible in the sky. Now, we are asked to imagine that both sides of these steps are adorned with flowers and other ceremonial objects. We are told that this is a very special night. We imagine that this is the night for which we have been preparing over the past months, or perhaps even years, that we have spent in this plaza. We have finally earned the right to climb these steps tonight by having completed our task of releasing all our former beliefs and attachments that have tied us to our old way of dreaming our life. We have now come to the point where we are willing to give up our physical form, if necessary, in order to transcend into our true nature as pure Spirit! We don't know what fate lies for us at the top of these steps. We know we are finally willing to jump into the unknown. When we jump, we are warned that we won't be able to see into the darkness. Since the night is so dark, we won't be able to see whether we will jump into life-saving water or whether we will land on solid stone. We just know that we are now willing to physically die, if necessary, to experience what we truly are as spiritual beings.

For this next step, we must recognize that our basic truth is the pure essence that we are. We are so much more than our physical bodies, and now we must recognize what remains after we peel away the illusions of our old beliefs. We must understand that our true essence is light, energy, and spirit. Our essence is life, and our very presence is the truth. The truth existed before our mind was formed. It exists without belief. Now we must choose truth instead of limiting beliefs in order to take this step toward our freedom. The biggest obstacle in this moment is to recognize our fear and decide to go forward anyway.

As we open our eyes and peer up to the top of the steps, we are asked to ascend the steps whenever we are ready. After some contemplation, I begin the steep ascent. When I reach the top, I am greeted by the amazing beauty of the Temple Pyramid of Quetzalcoatl. The Temple is adorned with beautiful stone sculptures featuring the head of the Feathered Serpent. Each of the Quetzalcoatl heads on the side of the Pyramid has an open mouth. Don Miguel explains that, in ancient times, the temple priests would randomly release water through the mouths of these Feathered Serpents. This would be done just before the night when the acolyte's ceremony would be held. Either the area below would be filled with water, or it wouldn't be. Without the reflective light of the moon, it would not be easy to tell. The acolyte would have to be ready to forfeit life in order to jump into the mouth of the Feathered Serpent.

I look around me from the top of the steps. I can see how this view appears like the open jaws of a serpent, with me standing on the edge of the chin before the open mouth. When we are ready, don Miguel asks us to imagine jumping into the open jaws, as if we can't see whether there is water below to catch us or not. This act of power signifies our faith that no matter what happens, we can trust life to guide us into the unknown and that our authentic essence is not our body. We are the force that moves matter — the force that moves our body — and we have always been this force.

Standing on the edge, I contemplate my jump. I become aware that there are two possible outcomes. In one outcome, I find that there is no water below to soften my fall. My body is broken by the impact on the stones below, and I become free from this body. I fly upwards in sweet gratitude as a pure spirit. In the other outcome, I land in the water. I feel very grateful for my life and my body. However, I now understand that I can truly know myself as pure spirit, even though I am still in a body. I have conquered my fear of losing my body and releasing my old beliefs about who and what I am. Both outcomes lead to the same result. I am surprised that I can see this is so, and I acknowledge how powerful that understanding actually is for me now.

After we have taken this imaginative jump, we are encouraged to enter the Temple area below and contemplate our choice to release our old life and attachments. I walk back down the steps and enter through the opening on the right side of the pyramid. I take a seat on the steps inside the temple and meditate for a while about my choice to go for personal freedom and leave my old attachments behind. I notice that for each Feathered Serpent head on the side of the temple, there is another symbol next to it with two open circles for eyes. Although the Aztecs have called this figure Tlaloc the rain god, don Miguel says that this figure was (long before the Aztecs arrived) originally meant to represent Tezcatlipoca (also known as the Smoky Mirror), the twin of Quetzalcoatl. That is why both twins appear together on the side of the Temple.

I understand that, in Toltec teachings, Tezcatlipoca represents the black light, the pure unmanifest energy, the void, and the nagual — the formless source of pure potential and pure Intent. According to don Miguel, the Toltecs knew that most of the energy in the universe exists in this unmanifest form. In contrast, Quetzalcoatl represents the white or visible light. It is the manifest side of creation, the tonal. Both are essential for the creation of the universe that we experience. Together, they are the yin and yang of genesis.

As I meditate here, I feel the powerful dance between these forces in creation. I am particularly drawn into the two circles of the figure of

Tezcatlipoca. It feels as if there is a magnet pulling me into "the eyes of Intent." I experience the vast space of the void, the darkness filled with powerful energy and potential. At the same time, I feel surrounded by a loving energy. I feel seen by the darkness within those eyes, and I feel deeply acknowledged.

According to Carlos Castaneda, in the Toltec teachings, Intent is a force that exists in the universe. It has nothing to do with the mind, although it can be experienced. The mind can have an intention. But Intent is not a thought, an object, or a wish. It is the force that "impels a shaman through a wall, through space, to infinity." Castaneda says that it is the eyes that focus this force. As I sit on these steps today facing the Temple of Quetzalcoatl, I feel the focus of those two circles in the figure of Tezcatlipoca opening a space of the infinite within me. I notice how I can perceive both sides of the void at the same time — the manifest dances within the unmanifest, and vice versa. I sit here in a physical body, peering into the depths of the infinite. Such a sweet vision!

Before leaving the area, we are offered an opportunity to peer into the darkness inside one of the Feathered Serpent's open mouths near the Temple exit to experience the vast potential of the void, or the universal womb of creation. After completing my contemplations, I wait for my turn to peer into the void of the Feathered Serpent's open mouth. As I look inside, I feel the vast openness of new possibilities and the start of my expanded adventure into Spirit. I'm amazed by how vast the darkness within this small opening appears. It's as if the ceremonial releases and the meditation I have just completed have created an open expanse within me that I can perceive reflected in the depths of this darkness. I imagine healing water pouring forth from this darkness within that cleanses my body and soul inside and out.

As I leave the Temple of Quetzalcoatl, I join a few friends. Together, we walk back through the dusty Sea of Possibilities. I imagine all kinds of potential beliefs floating around in the Sea, just waiting for a human to choose them and become attached. I see how these beliefs become like a weight belt that will hold them as prisoners within the Plaza of Hell. For the moment, I am grateful to have released some of my own beliefs that previously held me there. I feel much lighter, yet surprisingly exhausted. All the work we have done this first day in Teotihuacán, not to mention the previous full 24 hours it took to get here, have truly left me drained and exhausted. My friends and I head back to the hotel, Villas Arqueológicas Teotihuacán, for a much-needed and well-earned rest.

Before dinner that evening, we gather in the biblioteca to share and more deeply integrate the experiences of the day. Everyone finds a seat on the floor or the cushioned benches lining the room's edges. We begin with an opening prayer of gratitude for life and for the many blessings that we have received. I am anxious to hear what my friends want to express about their experiences from the day and to hear everything that don Miguel has to say to us. Some of my friends speak of having profound meditations while sitting before the Temple of Quetzalcoatl. Others share how powerful it was to examine ways the people and material things of their life had made them feel secure in their beliefs and how hard it was to release them.

With don Miguel's guidance, we examine our experiences. He cautions us to not waste our time using words to describe our experience. Instead, he recommends that we should just be open to any experience without words. Without words, we can perceive an experience on many more levels and dimensions than is possible through words. Without words, the voice in our head stops, and we can realize all the levels of reality. We can then access the Silent Knowledge that is far beyond the ability of words to describe.

Don Miguel continues his teachings. Today, he notes that we have released a big part of our personal story. We examined old beliefs that have made us feel safe in our life. We have lived a long time in an old story that was never as real as we believed. It has always been a dream. In truth, we know now that we exist without the story and even without our physical body. When we chose to jump into the mouth of the Feathered Serpent, we chose an act of power that acknowledged the truth of what we are: alive and powerful beyond the dream.

This evening, don Miguel again emphasizes that we are the force that moves our physical body, but we are not the physical body. From the human point of view, that force is undefinable; we don't even truly understand how it is possible to move our hand, blink an eye, or even think! We basically take those things for granted. Yet, when we finally understand that what we truly are cannot die, this understanding will lead us to the ultimate freedom to live our lives according to our truth. Our physical body will eventually perish, but there is nothing that can ever hurt the real life within us. We are Life itself!

Here in Teotihuacán, we are learning how to move beyond the dream — the conditioned and deeply programmed responses that are familiar, comfortable channels engrained since our childhood. The old outside dream has a gravity that is hard to break free from. Yet our true purpose in life is to realize our truth, not to live in lies that are built on illusion. Our essence is divinity, and it always has been. To live in love is our highest purpose.

The reward achieved when we live our lives in truth is to experience Heaven on Earth with every breath. We choose love over fear because we can see that the path of fear is always a dead end.

And now, let's go enjoy a wonderful dinner!

"Who can tell what miracles

Love has in store for us

If only we have the courage

To become one with it?

Everything we think we know now

Is only the beginning

Of another knowing that itself has no end.

And everything we can now accomplish

Will seem derisory to us

When the powers of our divine nature

Flower in glory

And act through us."

- Iqbal, Sufi Mystic

Plaza of The Earth

Chapter IV

Rebirth in the Place of the Women

I awake on the second morning feeling refreshed. I feel lighter, as if something heavy has been released. My morning shower feels exceptionally warm and cleansing. As I step outside my door onto the walkway surrounding the central swimming pool, I notice the beautiful magenta bougainvillea gracefully flowing in the breeze above the pool's turquoise water.

I hurry to join our group in the hotel restaurant for breakfast. This morning, I have a little more time to visit with friends and enjoy a breakfast of salsa verde huevos rancheros and coffee. I feel such delight reuniting with my fellow apprentices. There is always so much joy in being together. Many of my fellow apprentices have been to Teotihuacán before, so they can answer my questions and my curiosity about what will be in store for us in the coming days.

After breakfast, we meet again in the biblioteca, where don Miguel provides his powerful insights and instructions for the coming day. Everyone finds a seat on the floor or the cushioned benches lining the room's edges. As don Miguel speaks this morning, sometimes his words are profoundly accentuated by loud explosions from the neighboring village of San Sebastian

Xolalpa, Teotihuacán. The explosions create a surprising emphasis to his words and add a magical dimension to our surroundings. Our adventure already seems to be filled with explosions on many energetic levels that seem, through their power and emphasis, to open an even more expansive window in my consciousness to the spiritual dimensions. With an occasional sly pause in his words, it seems as if don Miguel has planned this extra element to help shift our normal perspective to a more conducive elevation. With each explosion, my perspective shifts slightly to allow his words to touch a deeper place beyond my reason.

Today, don Miguel explains that we will have a ritual that will give us a greater depth of appreciation of Life. Yesterday, we chose to take a step that required a personal act of power by jumping into the mouth of the Feathered Serpent. We were willing to let go of the prison of illusion into which we had bound ourselves. By taking this action, we recognized ourselves as pure spirit. We made a choice to let go of the beliefs that had been the guiding force of our previous life because those beliefs no longer serve us. We know now that those beliefs were based on illusions and fear. They were part of the outside dream, the Dream of the Planet, that existed before we were born. During our lifetime, we came to understand that they were necessary because they provided a foundation upon which we could structure our lives. But in truth, our beliefs had prevented us from understanding who we truly are as powerful, creative, and loving beings.

In Teotihuacán, the central road representing the body of the Feathered Serpent is known as "The Avenue of the Dead". It is called this because, in Toltec teachings, only the "dead" are allowed to cross the river (a creek in today's reality) that divides the southern part of the site from the rest. After we take the jump into the mouth of the Feathered Serpent, in a symbolic way, our past is no longer alive to us. He tells us that, as we continue our journey through the body of the Feathered Serpent, we will be assisted by the serpent itself, as it helps to burn away (and metabolize) every part of our old belief system that does not serve us as beings of light. By the time we emerge from the other head of the serpent, which is the Pyramid of the Moon, we will know ourselves as Pure Light! We will still have our bodies, but no longer be trapped in our old beliefs that no longer serve us.

As I sit cross-legged on the floor among friends I love, how beautiful I imagine that new dream to be! I decide to give my full faith and intent to my process here. I affirm to myself that I will put forth my full effort and my faith in allowing Teotihuacán to assist me on this journey to Light.

The ritual that we are to experience today will be to imaginatively attend the funeral of our physical body so that we can rebirth a new dream for our life. We begin this ritual with a meditation as we sit in the biblioteca. As spirit, we are to envision who will be coming to our funeral, especially our friends and family. We need to have so much gratitude for our physical body because this body has served us so completely in every way. It has always done everything we asked for, as well as it possibly could. Perhaps we did not always treat it well and took it for granted. Maybe we sometimes thought it was not perfect, according to our concepts of perfection. We are also asked to envision our family and friends at our funeral, to hear what they say about us, and to have so much gratitude for every way they have contributed to our life experience, whether we consider their contribution to have been for better or for worse.

After some time for contemplation and envisioning, I quickly collect the things from my room that I will need for the day—my hat, water bottle, and backpack. Again, we walk together to Puerta 1 and enter the sacred site. Since today is Sunday, entrance is free, and tickets are not required. I follow the group as we pass the row of shops leading to the Visitor's Center. Stepping down from the Visitor Center steps, I see, at a distance, the wall facing us that surrounds the "Plaza of Hell", where we were yesterday. Today, instead of walking straight toward that wall, we turn left and begin walking north along the Avenue of the Dead.

As we approach the bridge over the small river or small creek, I notice some of my companions stop to kneel briefly and touch the earth in recognition of this sacred crossing. As I do the same, I express my gratitude and experience a feeling of reverence. I recognize that only my willingness to focus my intent on being as true to my journey as possible and doing my best here will allow the serpent and Teotihuacán itself to assist me.

We walk a little farther past the "river", and I see my friends, who are just ahead of me, bend down to touch, and some even kiss, the first step of the wall surrounding the first plaza, which don Miguel calls "The Plaza of Earth". It was such a sweet act of honor and gratitude that I again chose to do the same. When I climb the steps to the top of the wall, I overlook a rectangular plaza, much smaller than the one we entered yesterday. This plaza is about the size of a full city block. In the center is a small platform that is similar to the mesa in the center of the plaza we visited yesterday, but this mesa is much smaller. It seems clearly to have eroded over many centuries and deteriorated from its original shape, although it was never as big as the Island of Security in the Plaza of Hell.

Standing together on the top step, we are introduced to the Plaza of Earth. Don Miguel explains that this area also represents the human mind, as does the Plaza of Hell. But here, it reveals how our mind has already begun to change for us, those who have chosen to release our old beliefs and begin the passage through the body of the Feathered Serpent. The central platform still represents our Island of Security. But it is much smaller because many of our old beliefs no longer seem as solid and secure as they once were. The Island of Security is deteriorating and releasing its hold on our minds! We no longer need a big platform created by our beliefs to make us feel safe. Don Miguel tells us that the smaller island signifies that our knowledge has been wounded, and its power is now less controlling because we are no longer prisoners of our beliefs. However, we do not need to kill knowledge if we can learn to use it as a tool. It can still serve us as long as we do not allow ourselves to get caught in its web as we were before. The purpose of knowledge for us from now on will be primarily to communicate with our fellow humans.

We have come here to have our funeral. We each select a spot within the Plaza of Earth and take several minutes to complete our personal funeral celebration. We take time again to imagine everyone who will attend, what they will say about us, and what our life meant to them. We give thanks to our physical body and all the things and people in our life who have been a part of our life journey. After completing our imaginary burial rituals, we gather again at the top of the wall on the left side of the plaza. We learn that, after having buried our old self, our new self must now be birthed.

We walk together along the top of the wall, passing out of the Plaza of Earth. We turn to our left and follow a path, passing a cool grassy area with some Pepper Trees offering shade. It isn't far before we arrive at the "Place of the Women". We pass through a stone entrance and walk down a few steps into a below-ground chamber. Here, we walk along an elevated walkway with rope guidelines. We come to a deck area on the right of the path. Each person finds a place to sit and prepare for our birth process to begin. Several women act in pairs as midwives, taking turns until we each have been "reborn".

One by one, after our birth, we are led a little further along the walkway to the "shower" area. At this spot, to the right of the walkway, is an open alcove with a pipe exiting the rock wall above my head. I take an imaginary shower with some help and energetic cleansing from two other women. It does feel refreshing, even though there is, of course, no actual water. A few steps past the shower, I notice an iron cover over what appears to be a well. The women I am with open the heavy cover, and we peer down into the well. The opening is about two feet in diameter, and the sides appear to be made of cut rocks, as are almost every wall and structure at the site. I see only darkness in the depths—not any water as far as I can see—but the smell is very earthy and a little dank. One of my companions explains that don Miguel once suggested to her that this well has an energetic link to the area he calls "Heaven", which is near the feminine Pyramid of the Moon. She explained that, in the Toltec mythology, the Pyramid of the Moon is an energetic portal that draws new "spirits" wanting to be born in human form. Those spirits then travel through an underground energetic channel to the Place of the Women, where they are birthed into a human body.

We turn and follow the elevated pathway around a curve and then back toward the entrance. I look around me and notice how much this area reminds me of a dream I had about a year earlier. At that time in my life, even though I had been apprenticing with don Miguel, I wasn't sure whether I could ever actually come to Teotihuacán because of my work and family responsibilities. However, I often dreamt of being together with don Miguel and the other apprentices in our group. In one particular dream, I remember a space very similar to this one.

Along with several others in my dream, I am standing in about a foot of shallow, clear water. We are placing stones to build part of a temple or sacred space that seemed to be partly underground, just as it is where I am now. I find it interesting to have dreamt about a place so similar. Until I arrived here, I didn't know that Teotihuacán was built from many, many stone walls, floors, and chambers. The resemblance of this place to my dream is very striking. The water in my dream is also interesting because I have learned since then of many ways that water has significance here in Teotihuacán. Although this part of Mexico is now semi-arid, I keep getting a feeling that in ancient times, water was more plentiful here than it is today, and some parts of the site appear to have been designed to accommodate flowing water.

My two companions and I walk back to the entrance of the Place of the Women. We follow the pathway back toward the grassy area near the pepper trees. Our fellow apprentices are relaxing there in the shade after their rebirth experiences. Here, don Miguel tells everyone that we are now like newborn babies. We must begin to see life through new eyes. It is important that we take this opportunity to change and restructure the way we dream and experience our life from this moment forward.

After our funeral and rebirthing experience, everyone seems happy and exhausted! I am amazed at how much energy it requires to take part in these simple ceremonies here in Teotihuacán. After everyone has completed their rebirth, we walk back to the hotel in small groups to prepare for our evening meal at a nearby family restaurant that we lovingly refer to as "La Comadres", although its actual name is El Mirador.

"In the depth of my soul

There is a wordless song."

- Kahlil Gibran

Open field near the plazas

Chapter V

Exploring the Plazas of Water, Air, and Fire

On the third morning, I awaken to a series of explosions that seem to be coming from the neighboring community. I have been hearing these explosions in the distance for the past couple of days, but they are happening a little more frequently each day. At breakfast, I ask my friends about the explosions, and they explain that the local community of San Sebastian Xolalpa is preparing for the upcoming feast day of their patron saint, Santario de San Sebastián Mártir. Although the feast day isn't until January 20 (still a week away), the community begins celebrating with firecracker explosions days in advance.

After a boisterous gathering for breakfast in the hotel restaurant and our group meeting in the biblioteca, we again prepare for another long day at the site. Today, we follow our usual path to Puerta 1. We wait at the edge of the parking lot while don Miguel and Gini purchase our entrance passes. As we walk through the gate, our tickets are stamped on the back with "ene 13", which I realize is the Spanish abbreviation for January 13.

Today, we again turn left up the Avenue of the Dead and pass over the river. This time, Gini leads us through the Plaza of Earth until we climb the steps at the far end. Here, we pause, looking over another very similar plaza but without a mesa or anything in the center. Gini explains that we are overlooking the "Plaza of Water".

In Toltec teachings, as in many other traditions, water is associated with emotions. In many ways, emotions are like water. When it is unimpeded, water flows just as our emotions flow when we allow them to move through us in a natural way. A young child can be furious one moment and joyful a few moments later. Most young children do not hold onto their emotions for long. This is our natural approach—until we learn to create stories and judgments about ourselves and our emotions that make it hard to let them go.

This is especially true for fear-based emotions because it's as if they become trapped in our emotional body. They are like poisons that often lead to problems with our health, even years later. Perhaps this is because, as don Miguel has explained, "Only love feeds our soul". Other emotions are not as easily released. Imagining emotions to be more like water helps us to cleanse and heal our emotional body.

I think back to the time don Miguel spoke to us during our first Circle of Fire Ceremony, held in Grass Valley, CA, saying: "I want you to be like water." He noted that water has no resistance. It has no shape of its own. It flows through a space and fills every crevice, flowing over and around every obstacle. It exists as a solid, a liquid, and a gas. As humans, we are also matter, soul, and spirit. When we begin to understand ourselves in this way, we can move through life with greater ease and grace.

Flowing water can help us release old emotional poisons, which may have been the original symbolic purpose of water baptisms. Water cleanses both our physical and emotional bodies. Immersing ourselves in water can be refreshing, relaxing, or energizing. Our bodies are made mostly of water, which is essential for all living things on Earth.

Research initially performed by Dr. Masaru Emoto has shown that the very structure of water crystals can be influenced by our thoughts and emotions. In his study, water subjected to positive emotions and words led to beautiful and symmetrical crystal shapes when frozen, while water subjected to negative emotions and words resulted in more irregular patterns. Although more research is needed, at least one subsequent, double-blind study performed by other researchers also indicated that sending positive intentions from Japan to water samples in California resulted in "higher aesthetic appeal" than the crystals of the control water.

Since our bodies are mostly made of water, the connection between emotions and our physical well-being is direct and dynamic. To me, this research really "brings home" the importance of cleansing and releasing any anger, sadness, or fearful emotions that we have been knowingly or unknowingly holding on to. Here in Teotihuacán, in the Plaza of Water, we have an opportunity to use our imagination and Intent to help us with this deep release.

When we move through this plaza, we are encouraged to employ our imagination to allow the properties of water to provide purification to further cleanse away any remnants of emotional burdens, old agreements, and beliefs that no longer serve our highest Truth. We can allow the water to cleanse and purify our body, mind, and spirit. We can permit the water to flow through all the crevices of our mind and begin to deeply release past traumas and heaviness that we have held in our emotional body. As we walk, we allow the water to cleanse and purify our body, mind, and spirit. We will then come together again when we climb the steps at the far end of the plaza.

Several times during our apprenticeship, don Miguel has explained that emotions are the bridge between our body and our soul. Emotional trauma or pain leaves an imprint that remains until we use our awareness to meet it with understanding, love, and forgiveness. Without awareness, we may carry this imprint within our emotional body, and it often affects how we relate to our life experiences. In order to bring this into our attention and awareness, our life provides a mirror that reflects the pain we are holding, offering a new experience or opportunity to resolve the hurtful emotional imprint. Without awareness, we often react to reinforce the pain rather than releasing it. We then usually create a story about how difficult life is, never realizing that life reflects what we hold within us. This story that we create reveals how our word and our faith results in the way we experience our reality. This is essentially confirmation bias; our experience reflects our beliefs, and our beliefs reflect our experience.

Today in the Plaza of Water, we have an opportunity to align with Intent — the unknowable force — to help us release old imprinting and cleanse our emotional body. With the help of Intent, the gift we receive through this simple act of walking through the plaza can be more profound than our cognitive reasoning mind can comprehend. Old, imprinted emotional patterns can be cleansed, loosened, or even transformed. In my experience, taking myself completely out of the process, surrendering to Intent, seems to dramatically enhance the power of cleansing and transformation, beyond what my reasoning mind could ever devise.

As I begin to walk through the Plaza of Water, I align with Intent and imagine that I am moving effortlessly through clear and gentle turquoise waves that wash all around me, cleansing and clearing away all the remaining energetic bits of the old beliefs and agreements that I have been working to release over the past two days in Teotihuacán. I choose not to go straight across, but instead, I weave and dance through the water, sensing the joyful release of everything that I no longer want to hold and carry in my emotional body. As I reach the end of the plaza, feeling refreshed by my immersion in the water, I climb the steps to get a view of what adventure will come next.

The next plaza is similar in size and has a large pyramid-shaped stone structure in the center. I learn that this area is called "The Plaza of Air." We stop here, overlooking the plaza, to consider the symbolism of air and how it relates to our lives and to many of the Toltec teachings.

Air is breath, and breath is essential to life. The element of air also represents spirit. This has been true in many cultures for millennia. I remember how almost every ancient statue that I saw in Egypt appeared to have their nose hacked off. I learned that this was because those who wanted to destroy the spirit of a being represented by the statue believed that by destroying the nose — the source of breath and, therefore, life — they rendered the statue lifeless. Thereafter, breath of air and life could no longer remain, and whatever powers the statue represented would be revoked.

Air and breath can be a powerful healing force. When we are angry or hurt, we almost unconsciously hold our breath for a moment, and then we may begin to breathe harder or faster than normal. It helps to stop and focus on our breath for a few minutes before speaking or taking action. Pausing this way can help us get centered and calm, giving us a better approach in the moment. "Before acting in anger, take deep breaths and count to ten." Is certainly good advice.

Yoga exercises require using our breath to deepen and strengthen our stretch and help us hold a pose longer for greater benefit. Yoga breathwork can also be a powerful force in moving the energy through our body and releasing trapped emotions. In Toltec training, breathwork is essential in the process of recapitulation, which helps us reclaim our energy from all the experiences, people, and places in our life where we may have left some of our lifeforce energy.

The gentle or forceful movement of outdoor air becomes the wind. Wind can be playful, soothing, inspiring, life-giving, and sometimes destructive. Wind can dance, cry, howl, sweep, and whirl. Wind drives our weather, and on the grand scale, it is the turning of the Earth that keeps the air in our atmosphere constantly moving and dynamic.

In the Tarot, the element of air is represented by the suit of swords, meaning knowledge, action, power, and change. Don Miguel once explained that the sword represents truth, as it does in the story of Excalibur being pulled from the stone. In this story, only the one who is virtuous, just, chivalrous, and divinely called would be able to remove the sword. The Archangel Michael holds his sword high so that it can cut away anything that doesn't serve the highest good and conquer that which is evil. I also remember the Bible passage where Christ meets his disciple John after his resurrection. He spoke to John with a "sword on his tongue", meaning that he spoke with power and truth.

The concepts of breath, God, words, and spirit have been intertwined in meaning throughout many human cultures. According to Neil Douglas-Klotz, in the Aramaic language, the word that Yeshua used for God was the word "ruha", which is a feminine noun that can be translated as "breath" and/or "spirit". Douglas-Klotz further explains that Yeshua used the term "nesha" (neshama) to refer to a human individual breath or spirit as an inseparable part of the ruha, the greater breath, of God. A modern translation of the Book of John in the Bible begins, "In the beginning was the Word, and the Word was with God, and the word was God."

As we overlook this plaza, don Miguel reminds us that air and breath are most significant to our word. How we choose to use our spoken and written word is one of the most powerful tools we have in life. As we enter the Plaza of Air, he asks us to think about how we have been using our words. We are to meditate here about the times we have used our word against ourselves or others. We are to consider how we can better choose our words in the future to be more impeccable, truthful, and supportive of our highest Self.

I step down into the plaza and find myself drawn toward the pyramid structure in the center. I think deeply about how I have used my word in the past. I feel sad as I remember that I have not always used it in a loving way. Many times, I've thoughtlessly said things that were hurtful or not fully truthful. At times, I have used my word against myself or others in hurtful ways. I place my hands on the beautiful stone of the pyramid structure in the plaza and ask for assistance in using my words more carefully and lovingly in the future.

As I lean my back against the rock structure, I feel the solid connection of the stone as it connects me with the Earth. There is a calm, grounded feeling that penetrates my body through the physical connection with the stone. I am reminded about how don Miguel has recently asked us to become "laconic". That was a word I had not been familiar with. He told us it came from ancient Greece, where the Spartans practiced verbal austerity. We are encouraged to not only speak less but to speak more carefully and meaningfully. He encouraged us not to say anything at all unless it is something important that would be helpful and productive in the moment. He warned us to avoid gossip and not speak about anyone who is not physically present.

Part of this practice was to be utterly silent on Fridays, as much as possible. Practicing being laconic and silent on Fridays has been a powerful practice for me. This was always about strengthening my will. By nature, I tend to be somewhat quiet anyway, so I had worried that being silent more often might make others pay even less attention to me than they usually did. Even so, I had decided that wasn't nearly as important as developing my will to be more careful and considerate of the words I chose.

One challenge had become apparent at work on Fridays. I explained to my officemate that I would be silent on Fridays. However, it became a game for him to get me to speak. Because answering my work phone was a necessity even on Friday, my officemate would sometimes call me on the phone just to tease me. Since don Miguel has often explained that "petty tyrants" are a blessing because they offer us opportunities to practice our training, I know I can take my officemate's playful teasing in stride.

Glancing around the Plaza of Air, I feel grateful to be here, knowing how special it is to have this opportunity for support in deeply examining how I have lived, spoken, and related to my life. Most of all, I am very grateful to don Miguel for showing me that there is a more loving, respectful, playful, and rewarding way to live. I look upwards now and see some of my fellow apprentices climbing on the pyramid structure. First, I wonder how they got up there since the stone is smooth all around and without easy purchase. Then I think, "Oh, of course, they are up there doing that!" This group always has fun while approaching every barrier as a challenge to be met.

Soon, I notice that our group is beginning to gather on the northern steps at the end of the plaza. I give thanks to the Plaza of Air for its gifts in helping me examine how I have used my word, and I make a new commitment to speak very consciously and carefully going forward.

Instead of going into the next plaza on the Avenue, we are now led along the left side into an adjacent area where the wall has been broken to reveal an area representing the "underworld". In ancient mythology, the underworld holds great significance in many cultures. In human terms, the underworld can be thought of as the unconscious mind. Even though we may not usually be aware of the aspects of ourselves that lie "below" our conscious awareness, these aspects can powerfully drive our emotional responses and actions. In particular, our culture, in many ways, has encouraged sexual repression. We may hold unacknowledged and repressed wounds around our sexuality. Today, we are encouraged to rest here and contemplate our own "hidden treasures" — to open the door of our unconscious and reveal to ourselves what may have been lost or hidden from our conscious minds.

As I meditate here, I simply focus my awareness toward allowing that which is below the surface of my conscious mind to bubble up into my consciousness in its own time. I feel that it is important not to force this process. So, I choose again to continue strengthening and expanding my connection with spirit here in Teotihuacán. After a time of contemplation, we emerge from the underworld into the next plaza, where we are encouraged to touch the Rock of Sexual Healing. I observe several of my friends as they seem to have a powerful emotional release simply by touching this rock after our time of contemplation.

Of course, this fourth plaza represents the element of fire. As I enter the Plaza of Fire, I pause, looking around this area to consider how fire is significant to my transformative journey here in Teotihuacán. For me, fire relates symbolically to vitality, assertiveness, and passion — both sexual passion and our passion for life and creativity. Fire also purifies and burns away any impurities. The Greek word "pur" translates to "fire," and this is the root of the English word "pure". Fire is dualistic, representing both cleansing and destruction. Either way, it transforms. "The fire within" can be described in Toltec terms as the nagual, or the spark of life. In this sense, it is the passion from which all creation stems.

As I walk through this plaza, I experience the fire as an energetic force — a purging force that burns away impurities and negative energies. Here, I rejoice to receive further assistance in burning away whatever remains within me that no longer serves my highest Truth. In this moment, it doesn't seem to matter whether I know exactly what is being burned away. My trust in the process is enough. It simply feels as if a deep, cleansing release is happening. Today, I am glad to surrender whatever remnants of limiting beliefs still linger in my mind or energy field, including those of which I am aware of and those of which I am not aware.

I feel myself becoming wholly immersed in the purifying flames. But very soon, I hear that all the women are being called toward the low hill on the left side of the plaza. I see also that don Miguel calls the men over to an area above the right side of the plaza.

Gathering with the women, we begin discussing the significance of growing up as female and many things that we learned through our "domestication" regarding what it means to be a woman. We speak about how we were trained to behave and what we learned about what was acceptable and what was not. Some of the women spoke of sexual abuse they had experienced. All of us seem to agree that we have often felt less powerful or less important in many circumstances compared to the men around us. We explore how powerlessness was often imposed by ourselves as much as by others because of our cultural conditioning.

In my case, I had vowed for a time as a child never to grow up to be a woman. This was partly because it had seemed to me that girls and women just didn't get to have as many exciting adventures as boys and men were allowed to do. I preferred to play "King of the Hill" with the boys on the playground as they pushed each other off the snowbank rather than sit on the cold blacktop playing jacks or "pat-a-cake" games with the girls. Of course, not every boy agreed with allowing me to join them, so I was grateful for my friend Jeff, who was willing to play with me anyway. Often, we had to leave the group of boys and make up our own games, always finding creative and active games to fill our recess time.

After our separate discussions, all the men and women come together in the center of the Plaza of Fire. Don Miguel explains that in ancient times,

Teotihuacán was a place where men and women were respected equally, and each sex was celebrated for their unique characteristics and for how they each contribute to create balance within the family and culture. The Pyramid of the Sun, representing male energy, is physically larger compared to the Pyramid of the Moon, representing female energy. Yet, both pyramids reach close to the same elevation because the Pyramid of the Moon is located on the rising ground toward the north of the site. Finally, don Miguel encourages us to share hugs with each person of the opposite sex in gratitude for the valuable contributions that both male and female provide to our beautiful experience of life.

After our celebration in the fire, we are free to explore the site further this afternoon or to head back to the hotel for a much-needed rest. As I begin my walk back down the Avenue of the Dead, I stop to rest and meditate for a while in the Plaza of Air. I find a comfortable spot to sit on the ground with my back resting on the rock pyramid. Here, I have a beautiful view facing toward the Pyramid of the Sun. I feel a sweet exhaustion from today's activities, and it is especially lovely to connect with the ground again through the solid rock at my back. As I relax here, my attention is drawn again to the distant explosions of firecrackers in the neighboring village. It's as if we have a soundtrack that intensifies a little each day to highlight the transformation that I feel expanding within me.

I close my eyes and rest a bit. I imagine sending a grounding cord from the base of my spine to the center of the Earth. Sitting here on the ground, it feels good to connect with the Earth in this moment. Next, I imagine connecting a channel from the sun in the sky to the top of my head, allowing the soothing energy to flow down from the sun and fill me with its late afternoon warmth.

After a few minutes, I open my eyes gently and peer toward the top of the Sun Pyramid that appears directly before me in my field of vision. A beautiful vision emerges as I gaze toward the top of the Pyramid. In my vision, the top section of the pyramid rises slowly into the sky, and a brilliant light emerges from the pyramid's center. This light begins to slowly fill the space that has appeared between the upper sections of the pyramid. Then I see the light separate to form many small balls of light that I imagine might represent each of us who have come on this power journey with don Miguel. The balls of light float gently into the sky surrounding the pyramid. Next, all the balls join back together, forming a narrow band of light hovering in the space between the top sections of the pyramid. Suddenly, in a burst, the light expands outward from the pyramid and instantly envelops the entire Earth in a gentle flash of light!

It was such a beautiful vision. I feel as if I have received a gift to show me how the love, the energy, and don Miguel's teachings that we have come here to explore and experience will expand around the world as we go outward from Teotihuacán to share our love and the Toltec wisdom everywhere our future lives will take us.

"Love is your nature;

Don't resist what you really are.

You can improve your life just by

Expressing what you are,

Just by following the love

In your heart

In everything you do."

- don Miguel Ruiz

Plaza of the Pyramid of the Moon

Chapter VI

Releasing Our Etheric Double on the Pyramid of the Moon

The morning of the fourth day of our journey in Teotihuacán begins with a thunder shower and many blasts of lightning. When we meet after breakfast in the biblioteca, I am again amused and intrigued by how the explosions and rumbling thunder powerfully emphasize important points that don Miguel is making. This morning, he reminds us about the time when he visited Teotihuacán in early 1992. It was then when he first noticed that the quality of the light from the sun was beginning to change. He realized that this was the beginning of the transition from the Fifth Sun to the Sixth Sun, as was predicted to happen around this time by ancient Toltec teachings and prophecies and several other indigenous cultures in the Americas.

We are reminded that the Sixth Sun represents a shift in global consciousness to a more evolved state of being and a return to Spirit. As don Miguel has explained, the vibrational frequencies of the light from the sun are already changing, although the process will not be sudden. The light has begun to shift, but the changes will be gradual and may take decades.

The Fifth Sun has been characterized primarily by movement, described as the shaking of the Earth. The Toltecs referred to the Fifth Sun as "the Sun of Injustice". For the most part, it is the only period that today's humans have access to recorded history. This history primarily documents male-dominated wars and conflicts. During this time of transition between the Fifth and the Sixth Suns, their influence can be felt around the Earth. A great deal of upheaval is currently experienced in human culture, as humans find the transition changes very challenging. The old ways no longer suffice, but the new ways have not yet come into predominance.

The transformation to the Sixth Sun will affect all life on Earth, according to don Miguel. There will be a dramatic change in culture toward greater connection, cooperation, and spirituality for humans. The prophecies indicate a time of elevation in the collective consciousness and the rise of more nurturing, feminine forces. All this suggests that we are living in a time of powerful transformation. I listen attentively as don Miguel explains that we have come together in Teotihuacán to dream together and help initiate the creation of a beautiful new dream for humanity and the Earth.

As apprentices, we have all understood how don Miguel has labeled the "old" dream as the Dream of the Planet. Most humans alive today were born into this dream, and we were taught what to believe and how to behave according to the rules of this dream. We accepted it completely, and our personal dream eventually became a reflection of this outside dream. At first, we may have rebelled as a child, but we surrendered because there was no option. The Dream of the Planet is primarily based on fear. It grows strong as it feeds on human energy of fear. It takes a lot of focused personal power to break free. In Teotihuacán, we are learning how to recover our energy that has been held in beliefs and attachments tied to our old dream. These beliefs and attachments were reflected in the way we have experienced life. Breaking away from them is not easy, but it is necessary if we want to experience life in a more loving and creative way.

For me, this morning's discussion provides an even greater appreciation for our experience here and the deep personal transformation I have been experiencing in Teotihuacán. We are here not only for our personal transformation and growth but to participate in creating a new and beautiful experience of Life for all beings — a New Dream — a dream that puts into action don Miguel's powerful vision for humanity. This vision reflects the realization of the consciousness of the Sixth Sun and is the principle underlying the non-profit Sixth Sun Foundation.

Today, on the fourth day of our power journey, there is just one plaza left along the Avenue of the Dead for us to experience. I am feeling a mix of exhilaration and exhaustion after the dynamic experiences and profound depth of transformation I have already experienced on this journey. As we walk together to the site, I feel deep appreciation for don Miguel, my fellow apprentices, and the site of Teotihuacán for the support and complete embrace I feel in my experience of this journey.

After entering the site, we walk together over the river and pass through the first four plazas — Earth, Water, Air, and Fire — until we reach the Plaza of Recapitulation. I intuitively know that this final plaza may be one of the most significant plazas for assisting my desire for transformation. Here, I must give my full intent toward honoring and then deeply releasing any remnants of old agreements and beliefs that no longer serve my highest Truth.

For many months, I have been practicing the ritual of recapitulation according to the ancient Toltec process as taught by doña Bernadette Vigil and other Toltec masters. As part of our early apprenticeship, don Miguel had given us the task of making a list of every person we have ever known. That was quite a task in itself! We then used that list with loving intent to meditate on each person, one by one, using a sweeping breath to reclaim the energy we left with that person and return their energy back to them. In this process, we try to envision our surroundings during a particular time with each person as clearly as possible. The more clearly we envision each scene and remember our emotional reaction, yet observe it now with neutrality, the better we can retrieve any energy that we may have left there without awareness.

An important key in this process of recapitulation is to see the person and event with loving eyes and not get drawn into any negative emotions from the past. Through this loving approach, I found it possible to release unhealthy emotional attachments and regain my personal energy that is needed for greater health and well-being. As don Miguel explained to us, "Only love feeds our soul." Even though I may have had a fearful reaction with a person at a time in my past, I can now choose to see the situation with neutrality, love, and compassion for myself and others.

Simply seeing the truth of our life experiences is only the beginning of recapitulation. It is important to see not only what is true about our life so far, but also what is just a story that was never true. I know that I have believed so many stories about myself, about others, and about my experiences. But what is real? What is the Truth? If I am not the stories I have believed about myself, then what am I? So many times, don Miguel has said, "I don't know what I am, but I know that I am."

In this moment, as I walk through this Plaza of Recapitulation, I align with the force of Intent to help me release any remaining unhealthy energetic fragments from my energy field. I want to be clear and bring all my energy into the present moment because it is truly needed now. I know intuitively that I do not have to use my reason to understand exactly how this can work, but simply to have faith in Spirit that allows it to happen. As don Miguel has often reminded us, "Faith is believing 100%, without a doubt."

Today, I hold and acknowledge that faith within me. I know that I am a living force, with love at my core, and that force moves matter. It moves my body, my mind. And my emotions. The stories I tell myself about my experiences were never real. They were creations of my dreaming mind, but my emotional reactions to them are real. Through recapitulation, I can choose to create a new, more loving way to view my past experiences. My body and my emotions are part of the tonal—the physical world—but my essence originates within the nagual–that force that cannot be seen or touched. It is my faith that opens the door to acceptance and transformation.

Exiting the Plaza of Recapitulation, my view extends down the Avenue of the Dead toward the Pyramid of the Moon. The distance appears to be about a quarter mile. Each of us will walk the distance alone, all the while building something called our "Etheric Double". During our walk, we are to imagine giving everything to this double that represents our image of ourselves in this life. This includes our appearance, our attachments, our emotions, our beliefs, and everything we think is related to our old self.

I begin the long walk with a powerful intent. I ignore the many distractions of tourists and local vendors hawking their wares. I focus only on my own process of creating my Etheric Double. My mind pulls on each aspect of my life that has been important to me–the things I have thought were a part of me, but were only a story. I imagine a transparent being growing next to me as I walk, and I imagine filling it with more and more of these old attachments and illusions that were a part of my previous identity.

If I am completely successful, the Eagle — the being who comes to me when I physically die, according to the Toltec teachings — will be fooled. The Eagle will take my double instead of the real me to merge it back into the universal sea of energy. I will then be free to choose my own course. Life beyond life!

During my walk, I imagine my Etheric Double growing and growing in size as I offer it more and more images and attachments from my life. I am so engaged in my process that I barely notice anything else until I near the end of the Avenue. It is there that I first see The Rock. This large, carved stone seems to have its surface carvings and most features worn away over hundreds of years, even perhaps over millennia. It is taller than I am, with a circumference greater than my arms can reach around it. I sense a feminine, mystical quality within the stone.

I am not quite sure what this rock is, but I feel a definite pull towards it. For me, it almost has the feeling of a living being, like a huge beating heart. Perhaps it is the heart of Teotihuacán—it certainly seems that way to me. I walk up to the stone and place my hands on it. I immediately get a welcoming feeling of calm centeredness and connection. There is definitely something ethereal and magical about this stone. As I look down and to my left at the center part of the stone, an image of the number 42 or 47 seems to appear. I wonder about the meaning of this number and whether that is the number of people here with don Miguel in our group. I think that could be possible, although I haven't counted everyone. I imagine the stone could be acknowledging the importance of our purpose in coming here on this powerful journey.

Soon, I see that our group may be coming together again. I look around for them and see some of them gathering on the low mesa platform in front of the Pyramid of the Moon. I join them for a short ceremony in preparation for climbing the pyramid to release our Etheric Double from the top.

After the ceremony at the base, we begin climbing the pyramid. I find the steps challenging because each one is a very high step. I climb slowly up the steep steps and notice how don Miguel is already nearing the top. I think to myself that he must certainly be quite a strong climber! We finally all get to the top and have a short ceremony to release our Etheric Double. I find this release much easier than I expected, perhaps because I had already done so much work during my focused walk up the Avenue of the Dead and the past few years.

After releasing our Double, don Miguel says we are free for the rest of the afternoon. From the top of the Moon, I look back at the long avenue. From here, there is a fantastic and beautiful view of almost the entire site.

I climb partway down the steps of the pyramid and sit on one of the lower levels with some friends to rest. We are feeling happy and exhausted. It is wonderful to relax here, looking back over the beautiful vista toward The Avenue of the Dead and the valley beyond that extends to the mountains far in the distance. It is sweet to sit here together and share our wonderful experiences of the day.

"When you love with no conditions,

You transcend the dream of fear

And become aligned with the divine spirit,

The love of God, which is

The love coming out of you.

That love is life,

And just like the sun

It is shining all the time."

- don Miguel Ruiz

Women walking on the edge of the sun pyramid

Chapter VII

Visiting Heaven, the Portal, and the Pyramid of the Sun

Rather than entering the site through our familiar Puerta 1, on our fifth day, we take a longer walk along the road that encircles the site until we reach Puerta 3, the Moon Gate. A few members of our group who want or need to reduce their walking today have decided to come via local taxis instead of walking with the group. This third gate provides entry near the northwest end of the site, closest to the Pyramid of the Moon. As we enter the site, we walk past a long row of vendor booths selling souvenirs, hats, and local artwork. I make a mental note of booths that look appealing for possible places where I might later find gifts to bring home for my family and friends. I especially like the carved Pyramids of the Moon, the Pyramids of the Sun formed of obsidian and green glass layers, and the obsidian figures with the gold veins and tiny gold sparkles that especially reveal themselves when placed in the sunshine.

From this entrance, we are close to the area that don Miguel refers to as heaven. The official name of this area is the Palacio de Quetzalpapalotl, which can be translated as the Palace of the Butterflies. Upon entering, we find a beautiful, open-air rectangular space surrounded by pillars and walls carved with pre-Hispanic mural paintings and carved stone reliefs. Several reliefs I can see feature the Eyes of Intent and stylized images of eagles with beautifully inlaid obsidian eyes. The upper areas of the walls still retain beautiful painted murals and reliefs showing ancient symbols and butterfly wings. Along a couple of the sides of the area, I notice recessed rooms with ropes across the entrance, allowing visitors to view but not enter the rooms.

We are asked by don Miguel to enter quietly to avoid disturbing the other tourists or drawing unwanted attention from the guards. In his experience, the guards have sometimes not allowed even an appearance of ceremony with groups. Our group gathered and waited for a few minutes along the wall to the right of the entrance until the center of the space was clear and other tourists had left. When it's clear, we each find a place to sit in a large circle on the stone floor around a small drain hole in the center of the open-air palace. A fellow apprentice quietly leads a meditation of gratitude and joyful appreciation for the gifts that we have received on this journey. Together, we softly sing a short song about holding a place for spirit in our heart. For me, this is a sweet and profoundly moving experience and a wonderful beginning for our day.

After a while, we rise and quietly leave the area. I follow the group as we walk a short distance to an open area directly behind the Palace of the Butterflies. This area is called the Palace of the Jaguars. Here, we enter an open courtyard featuring a series of rooms in a row along the northern side. As we walk in, I also notice that toward my left, there is an open entrance to several other partly restored rooms with partial walls but no ceilings.

In contrast, the series of rooms before me to the north are better restored, with three walls and a ceiling made from the corrugated tin that is common in restored areas of the site. The restored rooms all have a fourth side that is open to the courtyard. As I glance inside, the rooms appear to be empty but have partially restored murals on the walls. It's hard to be sure what the rooms contain because, as I stand in the sunshine, all I can see inside is a mystical, intriguing darkness that draws my attention with almost a feeling of reverence. I'm curious about the rooms, and one of my companions tells me that in ancient times, these rooms were where the high priests, ancient healers, and avatars once lived. I notice another similar room, just around a corner toward the left end of the row. My friend Barbara mentions that she has heard that don Miguel has explained that this room belonged to him at one time (perhaps in another lifetime?). Somehow, that feels quite possible to me.

I take a few minutes to stand near the opening of each room, one by one. I feel awe and reverence as I peer into the darkness of the rooms. They each seem to be about 20 feet deep and about as wide. I can barely make out the back wall from where I stand in the late morning sun. Although the rooms appear empty, they seem to me to be filled with an energetic presence, reminding me of how I have felt upon entering an empty cathedral, like the ones I had visited in Europe years earlier.

After a while, I notice that my friends are gathering in a line at the end of the row of rooms, waiting to enter another chamber. I walk down to where they are standing and hear that we are waiting to enter an area our group calls "The Portal". The guards are allowing about a dozen visitors in at a time. After a few minutes, our turn comes. We walk into a narrow pathway with a wall on one side and what seems to me to be a stage on the other. I wonder why a wall would be constructed so close to a stage, leaving almost no room for an audience. But, of course, the wall may have been constructed sometime during site renovations to protect the beautiful murals that I can see on the stage's back wall. It's hard to tell if this was ever meant initially to be a stage, anyway. So many things around the ancient site have been changed over the years.

Among my first impressions of this place is that it seems very sacred. I feel the energy surrounding me here to be both sweet and holy. A couple of guards are present to ensure security and quiet reverence for the space. My friends encourage me to gaze softly into the depths of the room at the back of the stage. Beautiful murals with reliefs in the shape of conch shells and other sacred designs border each side of the doorway to this inner room. Colors in hues of blue and pink and other muted colors bring the artwork on the doorway borders to life, while a more intricate story-like mural with bolder reds appears well-preserved on the front of the stage facing us. My friends explain that a figure of Christ or a holy being has appeared to others as they peer into the darkness of the doorway or opening that is beautifully framed by the artwork. In this context, my understanding of the word "portal" is a place of opening into other dimensions—a doorway to spirit—and to me, this place seems to be exactly that.

After a few minutes of appreciation, we exit the other door at the end of the Portal area. Stepping again into the bright sunshine, a friend explains that we must quickly head toward the Pyramid of the Sun. Apparently, don Miguel is already there waiting for us. I join a few other apprentices as we walk southward down the Avenue of the Dead toward the Pyramid of the Sun.

I am excited about this opportunity to finally climb the Pyramid of the Sun for the first time. In preparation for this event, don Miguel and others in our group have been discussing the significance of the sacred ancient ritual that we will participate in at the top of the pyramid.

One understanding that has particularly inspired me in these teachings is that each of us stands at the intersection between Heaven and Earth. We essentially live in the center of the circuit through which the Sun and the Earth "make love" to create life—the Life that we are. During the past few days, don Miguel has often reminded us of this by saying that we are the child of this union. We are the result of Father Sun and Mother Earth making love! How beautiful is that? As I have walked around Teotihuacán the past few days, I have often felt this energetic connection in my body very profoundly, very sweetly.

As we approach the steps of the pyramid, I remind my companions that we have been requested to climb it in a special, sacred way. This ritual dates back to ancient times. Climbing in this way provides us with even greater time for a physical and energetic connection with the pyramid, which ultimately helps connect us with its power and our intent for our purpose here.

This ritual starts at the right side of the steps, where I begin my ascent. I clasp my hands together behind my lower back. As I climb, I count twelve steps, moving a little to the left with each one. When I reach the twelfth step, I am on the left side of this section of steps. Now, I turn slightly to my right and climb twelve steps upward in this direction. This zig-zag process is repeated until I reach the first level of the pyramid, where there is a level space that surrounds the entire pyramid. As I climb, I occasionally notice that some of the Mexican visitors—primarily the older children—seem to be following the same ceremonial process.

When I reach the first of the three flat levels of the pyramid, I begin walking to my right, keeping my hands clasped behind my back. As a woman, I am to go to the right, counterclockwise, around the pyramid. I keep my gaze as far to the edge as I can safely walk. I am happy to walk along the level path for a while since my legs needed a break from climbing the many steps. As I walk, I soften my gaze, focusing as intently as possible at the very edge of the pyramid. As I do this, I have an almost intense vision of the stones moving faster on the downward side of the pyramid than the area of the level surface I am walking on. This sensation is rather disorienting in a mind-bending way. I feel like it's putting my mind in a kind of trance—or altered consciousness— although I find the feeling to be quite nice. I wonder whether doing this for the entire climb at each level might help to facilitate an expanded state of consciousness by the time I reach the top. I imagine this will help me prepare for our ceremony in connecting with my channel to the sun.

As I reach each corner of the pyramid, I stop and honor the direction according to my understanding of the Native American teachings concerning that direction. I choose the southeast corner as my East, representing sunrise, the light returning, renewal, birth, and new beginnings. The northeast corner represents the north with its cleansing winds, wisdom, ancestral knowledge, and introspection. The northwest corner becomes my west, where I stop to honor sunset, end of life, residence, and letting go. Finally, I reach the southwest corner, where I stop to honor warmth, childlike playfulness, and growth.

While I am walking counterclockwise around each level of the pyramid, I am passing the men in our group who are walking clockwise in the opposite direction. Sometimes, we offer each other a brief acknowledgment as we pass while remaining focused on our own inner processes during this sacred ceremony.

After I complete my counterclockwise circumference of the pyramid, I find myself back at the stairs and begin my ascension upward toward the next level area of the outer pyramid. I repeat my twelve-step zig-zag upward climb. I notice that this section of stairs is much narrower than the lower stairs, so I make each step to my left or right closer together to maintain my zig-zag pattern. When I reach the next flat area, I begin walking toward my right again along the outer edge of the pyramid. I'm amazed once again by the strange illusion of how the stones on the downward side of my vision seem to be moving so much faster than the stones at my feet or those to my left. I find this both beautiful and interesting. I know it's all about the way that my brain perceives the input of light in my eyes. I begin to think about how wonderful and amazing the connections between our eyes, brain, and consciousness are.

Soon, after climbing the final set of steps, I reach the uppermost flat area of the pyramid. I notice how much shorter it has become to complete the circuit of each of the four corners of the pyramid here on this highest level. When I return to the area of the stairs, I look back down toward the Avenue of the Dead, far below us. From here, I can see how the pattern of the stairs forms the shape of a person with arms stretched upward as if reaching for the Earth below. The legs of the image appear close to me, while the arms appear to reach downward. I imagine how, if I were very tall, standing at the top of the pyramid with my arms uplifted toward the sun, my shadow might appear just like this if it could be reflected on the side of the pyramid.

Now, I turn around and look upward toward the top of the pyramid. I see that most of our group is already there, sitting in various places amid the jumble of large rocks, similar to the area I had observed on top of the Pyramid of the Moon. Several people seem to be in meditation or contemplation, while others are speaking quietly in pairs or small groups. I notice that our group is scattered among several other tourists who have also reached the top. At first, I'm not sure how to join them since there are no stairs on this last part of the pyramid, and it is about five feet from the level surface to the top area that consists of numerous large rocks cemented together. As I stand there for a moment, I examine the slanted wall for the best way to gain footing on the smooth concrete surface that will enable me to scramble up to the upper level. Once on top, I look for a place to set my backpack. I find a place next to several others from our group.

I can see the entire site below from our vantage point on top of the pyramid. I can also see most of the entire valley and the mountains beyond. Some of the surrounding communities are also visible. I can certainly hear the frequent explosions coming from the community of San Sebastián Xolalpa as they continue to prepare for the celebration of their patron saint. I am awed and dwarfed by the beauty of everything I see, hear, and everything below that surrounds the Pyramid of the Sun on this early afternoon.

I feel such gratitude and aliveness to be here on top of the world with my friends. Soon, don Miguel summons us together to begin this special ceremony. He begins with a prayer of gratitude to Father and Mother God. I need to get very close to hear his words because many other tourists around us are talking, and the light wind partly obscures his voice. He reminds us that we are here to reclaim and reawaken our divinity by surrendering everything within us that is not of God. We are here to create a New Dream for our lives and for the planet—a dream of love without fear. We must claim our new life by reconnecting with the nagual that is within us—the unseen force that moves the universe, the force that moves the stars! He reminds us again that angel means messenger and that we are that angel, that messenger. Our life now will become our message. Our message is love and only love. From this moment, we must allow our actions to flow from our unconditional love that animates our bodies and the entire physical universe. We must be one with that unconditional love. Finally, comes the time for each of us to connect with our unique ray of light, that powerful energy channel to the sun!

As I hear don Miguel's last words, I raise my arms outstretched toward the sun. I feel the warm sunlight filling my body and connecting a powerful channel between myself and the sun. My mind begins to fill with golden sunlight until there is nothing in my conscious awareness except this ascendent light! For a few minutes, I experience only this powerful channel of light between me, the pyramid, and the sun. It's as if I could just melt into the sun, as if there is no distance, just pure connection. After a while, an image gradually appears in my mind within the golden light. I see a grandfather, an ancient medicine man, who welcomes me here in this ancient ceremony and tells me he is so happy to see me, his daughter, here again! I feel my eyes filling with tears at seeing him in my vision, and my heart overflows with joy, gratitude, and love.

Gradually, I begin to bring my conscious awareness back into my physical body. I begin to send a grounding cord from the base of my spine down, down through the center of the pyramid, and deep into the Earth. As I slowly begin to reconnect with Mother Earth, I consciously keep my connection with the sun and feel the energy moving from sun to Earth and back again. Everything around me appears as it was before the ceremony, but different, altered in some beautiful way that I can't quite define. The light around me seems more brilliant. I look around at my friends, and everyone seems a little changed. Some have tears; some are hugging. Don Miguel calls us together for a group hug, and we stand together for a long while, united in a New Dream for our lives.

Slowly, we part from our hug and begin to gather our things. I am almost surprised that my backpack is still exactly where I left it, even though it seems like almost an eternity has passed since I placed it there. I climb down onto the first platform before the stairs and begin the long, steep descent with a few friends. As we descend the stairs, we begin to sing one of our favorite songs: Row, row, row your boat…life is but a Dream!

Filled with an amazing lightness of being, I savor my descent and move a little slower than my friends. The steps are very steep, and I take them slow and carefully. It seems that I must concentrate and take care with every step due to the steep descent, and also because my expanded state of consciousness seems to have less connection with the physical world than usual. Everything around me seems to be filled with light and beauty! Everything sparkles in the sunshine, and the colors dance and move with an inner radiance! I realize now, in a powerful way, that how I perceive the world is truly determined by my inner state of being.

So often, my teacher, don Miguel, has tried to explain this to us, but I could only partially comprehend what he meant. For so long, it had been an ingrained habit for me to perceive the world as something separate from myself. I had found it hard to understand how completely my perception was controlled by habit and belief! Realizing that I can now always choose to perceive the world around me in this joyous and wonder-filled way that I am now experiencing makes my heart sing with joy and gratitude.

"Imagine one selected day struck out of

[your life] and think how different

Its course would have been.

Pause, you who read this.

And think for a moment.

Of the long chain of iron or gold,

Of thorns or flowers,

That would never have bound you,

But for the formation of the first link

On one memorial Day."

Charles Dickens

Side view channel of sun

Chapter VIII

My Walk in Conscious Radiance Toward the Angel of Death

When I reach the path at the pyramid's base, I turn to my left and begin to walk back down the Avenue of the Dead and toward our hotel. But I'm filled with a sweet resonance from the ceremony, and the radiant light of this afternoon beckons. I'm in no hurry to be anywhere in particular. I feel inspired to explore the site more since this will be my last opportunity before returning home tomorrow.

I haven't gone far before I see a wide, open pathway to my left as I pass the pyramid's corner. I'm intrigued to see what I might find there. I turn the corner and begin to follow this path. On my left is the Pyramid of the Sun. From this perspective, the pyramid seems to reach almost to infinity as I peer upwards. On my right are some partially restored ancient ruins. Looking further down the path, I notice an area with green vegetation that beckons to me. I imagine how nice it would be to rest there for a while and savor the light of the afternoon.

As I enter the area, I find myself in a small botanical park. I see that it is called Jardín Escultórico. It's a lovely sculpture garden with Teotihuacán artifacts. There are many beautiful plants here that I assume must be native to this area. Here and there, I find large ancient sculptures that must have been found elsewhere around the site and relocated here for display. Because I remain immersed in this wondrous state of boundless radiant consciousness, I spend an hour or more exploring the garden. I feel suspended in timeless beauty and wonder, losing all track of time. I commune with the exotic plants and allow my hands to connect with the energy of the ancient sculptures. I am especially intrigued by a giant ceremonial bowl carved of stone. It appears to be about three feet in diameter. I cannot see within the bowl. I view it from its side and bottom because its carved stone stand holds the bowl itself above my head. I imagine it must have been used in powerful ancient spiritual ceremonies and rituals. Although it isn't a deep bowl, it is certainly large enough to hold a generous amount of ceremonial substances.

After I've been enjoying the garden for some time, I realize that I haven't seen anyone else while I've been here. No other tourists, guards, staff, or anyone else seem to be in the area. I certainly feel very fortunate to be here now and to have this beautiful garden to myself.

Eventually, I find myself near a large carved stone head of Quetzalcoatl. I place my hands on the sculpture and feel as if there is a powerful ancient energy pulsing through the stone. I remember don Miguel saying that the ancient ones placed great knowledge and information in the stones. It seems now as if I was receiving some kind of energy transmission without words. The stone feels warm and alive. What I sense through my touch is almost a welcoming connection, a feeling of timeless awareness, service, and power. I don't know how else to describe it.

After a while, I look deep into the open and deeply weathered eye sockets and feel a kind, yet almost eerie, aliveness in the sculpture. I feel very blessed to have been allowed to connect in this way and be able to touch this wonderful sculpture and the others in this garden. Only after some extended time do I look down and see a small sign on a metal post nearby that says, "No Tocar." Although my Spanish is very limited, I suddenly feel that my consciousness has not been quite as aware of my physical surroundings as I usually am.

I give a little blessing of gratitude to the garden and step back onto the wide passageway along the south side of the Pyramid of the Sun. As I walk along next to the pyramid, I begin to notice what appears to be wide channels coming down from the upper parts of the pyramid. Although "channels" may not be the right word, I don't know what else to call them. The "channels" seem to be formed by large stone blocks that protrude from the side of the pyramid. Each one is at least eight feet or more wide, and several are set at irregular intervals along the pyramid.

As I move to stand near the base of one of these "channels," I wonder what their purpose is or was. It doesn't seem like they were designed to carry water off the pyramid since there isn't a smooth surface along them, because the blocks that form the pyramid are rectangular. This isn't an obvious design for channeling water. What purpose do these structures serve, I wonder? Standing here at the base of these structures on the side of the pyramid, it's as if I feel a massive rush of energy flowing down these structures. As a sort of test, I move off to one side just to see if it feels the same. But it doesn't. Without a doubt, I feel a great deal more energy flowing down these channels than I do standing next to the pyramid at another spot.

In my backpack, I have been carrying my fairly large Nikon camera. I have taken a few pictures in the sculpture garden, but very few others during this entire trip. Most of the time, I felt that taking photos during our activities would be inappropriate. It would either be too invasive, or else I was just too engaged with what I was doing to stop and focus the camera and adjust the light settings. But now, I think it would be interesting to take a photo at the base of one of these channels looking upwards toward the top of the pyramid. I wonder whether I will remember the feeling of cascading energy when I look at the pictures at home.

I take a couple of photos from the base of one of the channels. But after the second photo, my camera jams, and the film will no longer advance. No matter what I try, my camera no longer works. Why did this suddenly happen now? I've used this camera for years, and it has never had such a problem. Was the energy here next to the pyramid just too much for my camera to take?

Feeling a little disappointed that my camera isn't working, I walk a little further down the path. Suddenly, an interesting image appears in my mind. In this image, I see the Pyramid of the Sun in multiple images, one above the other. There appear to be about ten or twelve ascending levels of the same pyramid, each with a separation between them. Now, a kind of information transmission seems to come with the images. What I understood it to mean is that this pyramid exists in multiple layers of "dimensions." It is the same pyramid, but I can only see the one in "my dimension." I don't have any idea why this image and information suddenly came to me. Could it be related to the cascading energy I felt while standing near the pyramid's channels?

I think the idea of other dimensions is an interesting concept. I have never believed or not believed in the idea of multiple dimensions. I certainly know that my understanding of "reality" is very limited. Don Miguel has often instructed us that what we perceive as our "reality" is actually a virtual reality. I don't fully understand what that means, except that nothing is quite the way it seems. I don't even really know what I am, except I do know that I am so much more than I can comprehend with my mind. I know that I have experienced learning from don Miguel and being aware of his presence beyond this physical dimension many times in the past few years. So perhaps this pyramid, or all of Teotihuacán, also exists in other dimensions besides this one. In any case, I am grateful for receiving this image and for all the gifts I have been receiving here.

Suddenly, it dawns on me that the afternoon is already waning. It's still mid-January, so the sun is getting close to setting, even in central Mexico. No one in our group would have any idea where I am right now. I have not seen anyone I know since I came down from the pyramid a few hours ago. I hope no one is worried about me. A sign tells me that I'm not far from the Sun Gate, where I can exit the site and head back towards the hotel.

Soon, I'm outside the gate and begin to make my way across the parking lot to the perimeter road. I see that the sun is getting low. As I walk along the site fence, I pass a few restaurants and other businesses on the opposite side of the road. A few local people seem to observe me as if they think it strange to see a blond woman walking alone close to twilight. I walk and walk. I'm beginning to wonder how far it is back to the hotel and whether I can make it back before dark.

At one point, the path is broken by a small ditch with a bit of water at the bottom. I notice the partially decayed carcass of a dog in the ditch. The dog skull is very beautiful, I think. As I pass over the ditch, I hear a message in my mind: "The Angel of Death is very near." I wonder what this means, but I'm not particularly concerned. I still feel immersed in amazement and beauty from all I've experienced today.

Just as the sun dips below the horizon, I finally reach the driveway leading to the hotel parking lot. Approaching the hotel, I encounter don Miguel, walking with his stepson, Trey. Don Miguel gives me a big hug, and Trey hugs me from behind. Both of them squeeze me together in a warm embrace. At this moment, don Miguel whispers, "You are the beautiful Angel of Death."

Somehow, this makes perfect sense to me at this moment. I realize this was the meaning of the message I had just received: "the Angel of Death is very near." Everything I'm experiencing today seems part of a natural flow of magical and wonderful things. Many times, don Miguel has reminded us that the Angel of Death is our friend, and she is always near. Everything we have in this world, even our physical bodies, belongs to her. She helps us realize every moment's preciousness because every moment is a little death. In order to cross over the small river that flows across Teotihuacán, we first had to acknowledge that we have left our previous lives behind. Initiates of Teotihuacán have been told since ancient times, "Only the dead are allowed to cross the river."

After the big hug from don Miguel, I'm ready for a warm shower and a short rest before dinner. Our last evening is a time of celebration, sharing our personal experiences, and learning from one another about our most significant enlightened perceptions gained over the past few days. During our last meeting in the biblioteca, Gini, Trey, and others provided their insights about what we may expect to encounter when we return home. Tonight, I feel such a beautiful inner joy that I would love to continue to feel this way for the rest of my life. But I also understand the warnings we are being given tonight that there will be ups and downs as I return to my life and my job at home. I am warned that my family, friends, and co-workers will expect me to act like the person they have always known, even though I feel so completely different right now.

Most importantly, don Miguel warns us that we can easily be pulled back into The Dream of the Planet, which is still based in fear. We will be tempted to step back into our old roles and into our habitual behaviors and emotions. Now, we must remember that we can always choose between love or fear in each moment. If we don't like the way we feel, choose again. It isn't right or wrong. It's a choice. Our emotions are simply a reaction to the words we say to ourselves. Everything is action-reaction. We must be aware of the words we say to ourselves and how we describe our experiences. Only then can we choose with awareness.

In addition, he tells us that we will always understand the point of view that others generally accept within the old dream because we have lived there, but they will not understand us. Our family and friends will see and hear only what they choose to see and hear, according to their usual habits and expectations. They will want us to be as they have always known us. They will treat us that way, and we will be tempted to react as we always have.

It is not our responsibility to change them; we cannot change anyone else, just as we cannot live their lives for them. Every dreamer dreams in his or her own way. We must respect their dreams and show them our love without losing ourselves. We must be true to ourselves and be willing to live in our integrity. Don Miguel reminds us that integrity comes from the word integer, which means "one." In truth, there is only one being, and we are not separate from the One. When we share our love with respect, we provide a clear channel and offer those around us the opportunity to feel the connection.

At dinner this evening, everyone seems to be celebrating. After eating, I make an effort to connect with various friends sitting at different tables in the hotel restaurant. I enjoy hearing their perspectives and insights. Our group certainly takes up almost the entire room, and I appreciate how the waiting staff give us space and time to connect and share. As we finish our meal, we each receive a note detailing our outstanding charges that will need to be paid before we leave tomorrow morning. As the room begins to clear out, I notice some friends moving into the adjacent room with a small bar, where everyone sits on cushioned benches along the walls to talk and order drinks or dessert. One last time, I hope to order my favorite dessert, profiteroles. This is a puffed pastry filled with ice cream and covered with chocolate sauce. It is a wonderful treat that I've never eaten anywhere else but here in this hotel.

As I leave the dining area to join them, I run into don Miguel at the entrance between the rooms. I express to him how grateful I feel for this amazing opportunity to come to Teotihuacán with him and my fellow apprentices. I tell him how valuable this experience has been for me, how connected I feel to this ancient site, and how swiftly the time to depart has come. He listens quietly and tells me that I don't have to leave yet. A whole new group is coming tomorrow, and he would like me to consider staying for another five days to assist with their experience. He says I can go to the airport tomorrow morning and change my flight.

I am truly surprised and grateful for this invitation. I certainly haven't been expecting to stay another five days! At first, I don't know what to say. But here is my teacher offering a beautiful, unexpected opportunity. At this moment, I am torn. My heart leaps with joy at the invitation, yet I know that my family and my job are expecting my imminent return.

In this moment, my dear don Miguel stands before me with this interesting opportunity! How could I possibly say no after everything he has taught me? I would also love to have more time here to explore and commune with the energy of Teotihuacán. I feel so happy, connected, and alive here. I realize that only the fear of possibly disappointing my family or my boss could hold me back. Yet, if I am determined to live in integrity with my connection to Spirit, then choosing fear in any form cannot be my choice. So, I tell don Miguel that I will stay as long as I can change my flight. He assures me that this will indeed be possible.

"There are only two ways

To live our life.

One is as though

Nothing is a miracle

And the other is

As though everything is."

- Albert Einstein

Chapter IX

Welcoming New Friends to Teotihuacán

Very few of us who are staying at the Villas Arqueologicas Teotihuacán are getting any sleep on this night or even into the early morning. I keep dozing off for what seems like a few minutes. Again and again, I am soon reawakened by a nearby explosion of firecrackers, followed by sounds of a nearby marching band with drums, trumpets, trombones, and mariachi music that never seems to end, even as the morning light begins to appear outside my window. It seems as if I am hearing a constant parade that marches round and round the small town all night long. Don't they ever get tired, I wonder?

I am simply amazed that a celebration like this could possibly continue for hours and hours! I have never heard anything to compare with this. Even when the US celebrated its 200th anniversary a couple of decades ago, I'm fairly certain that the community festivies in towns all over the country were over, or at least much quieter, once midnight arrived. The celebration in this tiny Mexican town sure has a different approach.

I feel a little more concerned about my friends than about my own lack of sleep. They will be traveling most of the day today and will need to be awake and aware. After this long night of noisy celebration, they will most likely be exhausted before they begin their journey. The past few days of intense physical and emotional activities have already taken a toll on our energy levels. I am again amazed at how much physical and emotional energy this spiritual transformation work can take! Of course, we have been walking several miles each day, sometimes climbing pyramids and doing other physical activities. However, I wonder how much energy we have also needed for the processes of realigning our emotional bodies and our minds. I feel like so much has changed within me, and those changes must have needed energy beyond the physical requirements of my body.

For my part, I doubt that I would be getting much sleep during this night anyway. Right now, my mind is occupied by several concerns. How can I make sure that my flight will be changed correctly without speaking the language? How can I contact my family? (Note—cell phones were still very rare in early 1997, and calling from Mexico required going through an operator who may not speak English.) How can I contact my department (Environmental Health and Safety) at the university where I work? Will they be ok with my decision to stay twice as long as I had initially planned, since no one else is doing my job? What repercussions will I have to face when I do return?

Ultimately, I decide to trust Spirit and have faith that everything will work out fine, no matter what happens. I will simply do my best today to take the actions I need to take, step by step. I will not worry about the outcome. Depending on when I can schedule a new flight, I plan to be here through the next session, or at least the next few days.

The past five days have been so powerful for me. I now feel like a very different person in many ways. Today, I set my intention to keep my faith in Spirit, and to keep this intention even when I eventually return to my home and job. I don't ever want to waste everything I have gained and experienced here by simply returning to the way I previously experienced life. I feel a deep, joyful gratitude and an incredible zest for experiencing this new way of being in the world.

I am also grateful that so many of my friends and fellow apprentices have shared many experiences with me over the past few days. From our group discussions, I believe that we have each grown and changed immensely. I know that these friends will be valuable resources for me to turn to when I face challenges at home, and I plan to be a supportive resource for them, as well.

This morning, I wonder what it will be like when a whole new group of people arrive who have never worked directly with don Miguel as we apprentices have. I imagine that the high level of connection and elevated spiritual energy we've been experiencing will be totally different with the new group coming today. How could it be otherwise, since they may be new to these teachings? Some of them will essentially be learning everything from scratch. Others have already been working with a teacher who is an apprentice of don Miguel so they will understand a bit more. I think that everyone will probably be quite eager to meet don Miguel and be here with us in Teotihuacán.

Only somewhat recharged by my overnight respite, I finally get out of bed and dress for breakfast. This morning, everyone seems a little subdued in the hotel dining room, especially compared with our usual boisterous breakfasts and dinners. No one seems to have gotten much sleep, and most people have thoughts of international travel on their minds. In addition, we are all feeling a little sad about the impending departures. Many of us live in different places, although most live in California or New Mexico, where don Miguel has been holding many gatherings, mitotes, and apprentice training workshops.

After breakfast, I search for Gini to ask her whether I will need to move my things out of my room, even though I plan to return to the hotel after I get back from the airport later today. I find her near the hotel reception desk, where everyone is lined up to pay their bill and check out. She says I must vacate my room, return my key, and pay my hotel tab since new rooms and roommate assignments will be necessary once the new group arrives. Gini also informs me that Veronica, who is Federico's wife and one of the receptionists at the hotel, can assist me later today with making the necessary calls to my family and my department office at the university. That is a big relief!

Unexpectedly, Gini hands me a list containing names and flight information for everyone in the new group that will be arriving. She says it will be my job to check each person off the list as they arrive at the meeting place in the airport. I will need to explain to everyone what they need to know, such as where to exchange their money into pesos and where and when we will board the bus that will bring us to Teotihuacán and our hotel. I'm to answer their questions as well as I can, knowing that this whole experience will be very new to them.

This sounds like a big job to me. I don't even know what any of them will look like. What if I can't find them? I really don't know my way around the airport myself! What am I to do if someone doesn't show up? I remember how my friends and I were unable to make the planned connections during our own trip here. Gini assures me that the people arriving have been told where to meet the group at the airport and when to be there. She says that it's really up to them to be there at the designated time. Gini isn't one to coddle anyone, so the newcomers must be prepared to meet the challenges of international travel. The bus must leave the airport on time to bring everyone here to the hotel in Teotihuacán, so any stragglers who don't make it will have to make arrangements on their own.

I hurry back to my room, repack my suitcase, and get in line at the reception desk to check out. I request a place to leave my suitcase behind the reception desk, explaining that I will return for it later this afternoon. I keep an eye out for Betty and Judy to let them know that I won't be traveling back to Sacramento with them. When I find Betty, I ask her about leaving my car parked at her house for a few more days. She is surprised that I'm suddenly staying longer but tells me that her neighborhood is relatively safe, so my car should be fine where it is parked on the street in front of her house for a few more days.

By now, all the baggage for those departing is lined up in the hallways near the entrance, and everyone is outside near the bus, saying goodbye.

There is always so much shared love and respect for one another in our apprentice group. We all know that we will see each other again soon because don Miguel calls us together for apprentice training at least once a month. We also have our local "pods" that generally meet weekly to meditate and receive encouragement from each other as we practice the instructions that don Miguel has given us in our apprentice training.

When the time comes, I board the bus that will take us back to the airport. As it turns out, changing my flight is relatively easy, despite my concerns. As soon as that task is complete, I go to the meeting place at the airport. According to my list, several newcomers are already there, so I begin checking each person in. As I do this, I realize that this group sees me as a representative of don Miguel and the Sixth Sun Foundation.

Of course, they would—I'm the first person from our group to welcome them to Mexico! I hadn't thought of that until now, since other pressing concerns have been on my mind. I began to feel very blessed that they see me in this way. Of course, they have all traveled great distances from many places. Some of them have chosen to come on recommendations from their own teachers, who are don Miguel's apprentices. They have all heard good things about don Miguel and want to learn directly from him. His first book, The Four Agreements, has not yet been published—it is planned to come out later this year.

In my new role, I am happy to warmly welcome each person and ask if they have questions about changing their money or other concerns. We are waiting in an area not far from the Cambio (currency exchange) windows, but we have no seating available other than on the floor or luggage. Some group members are not scheduled to arrive for nearly an hour, so I tell everyone to get as comfortable as possible for the wait. I suggest that, if anyone wants to take a short walk in the airport area, they shouldn't go too far. I don't want anyone to miss the bus that will take us to Teotihuacán.

After the last flight arrived, there is still one man whose name appears on the list that I haven't yet seen. I ask everyone whether they know him or have any information about him. But no one does, so I hope he has contacted Gini or the hotel to let them know his status. When it's time for the bus, I gather everyone and walk with them to where our bus awaits. The driver is ready, and the motor is already running. He assists everyone in loading their luggage, and we begin the ride back to the hotel in Teotihuacán.

During the hour-long trip, I enjoy learning about some of my new friends and why they have decided to come on this new adventure. I'm amazed at how far some of them have traveled and how they have learned about don Miguel and his teachings. He has done a few local radio interviews, and a few articles about him have appeared in spiritually oriented magazines, but I'm not aware of any national publicity. (The internet doesn't yet exist for most people.) Apparently, the word has somehow reached these special people who are willing to undertake this new spiritual adventure in a foreign country.

As soon as I step off the bus at the hotel, I'm greeted by Gini. I give her the list where I have noted each new arrival, and then ask about the man who hadn't arrived at the airport. She replies that he called the hotel and will arrive later. Then, Gini tells me that, while the new guests are checking in and enjoying their welcome margaritas, don Miguel wants us to join him now in the courtyard near the pool.

Gini and I head to the courtyard right away. I find that a few other apprentices, including Peggy and Ted Raess, as well as don Miguel's stepson Trey Jenkins, are waiting at a table there with don Miguel. Gini and I sit down, and don Miguel asks each of us gathered here to put our hands together, one on top of the other, in the center of the table. As we do this, he invokes a blessing for us as we come together in service for the arriving visitors. Then, he asks us to lift our arms into the air with hands clasped together to signify unity and loving connection. I feel a power sweeping through me for a few seconds, and then it is done.

After all the new guests are settled, we gather in the biblioteca for an introductory meeting. Gini provides all the logistical information, and don

Miguel begins to explain how Teotihuacán has a long history as a mecca for spiritual visitors over thousands of years. He explains to everyone that Teotihuacán itself is now reawakening to support us in our connection to our own divinity, to our remembering and beginning to live the truth of who we are.

Many of our new friends are eager to express their delight in coming together with don Miguel in Teotihuacán. Some tell of recent dreams in which they experienced being here or being with the group and don Miguel. I am always amazed at how often people say that they have experienced don Miguel in a dream before meeting him in person. One man excitedly talks about a dream he had in the past couple of days. In this dream, he was in a hotel at night and kept hearing explosions. He goes on to say that the explosions led to a fire, and then he woke up immediately! I laugh at this, remembering all the explosions we have been hearing near our hotel the past few days, especially last night.

The other thing I find so intriguing about his dream is the concept of the fire and waking up. Isn't it the fire within- the burning desire within us- that spurs us to reawaken to a greater understanding of our spiritual nature? Certainly, don Miguel has used the symbolism of fire in many ways to inspire us to "wake up" from our old ways of dreaming and to burn away the old limiting beliefs that have never served us well. I'm amazed at how powerfully this new group of humans seems to be already connected to our purpose here in Teotihuacán!

I look forward to spending the next five days here with them.

"You have to stalk your own reactions;

You have to work with yourself every moment.

It takes a lot of time and courage

Because it's easier to take things personally

And react the way you always react."

- don Miguel Ruiz

Woman looking into mouth of Quetzalcoatl in temple

Chapter X
Revisiting Hell from a New Perspective

In our first morning meeting with the new group, after some of the logistics are covered by Gini, don Miguel explains about the light from the sun changing in this time as the transformation into the Sixth Sun begins. He reminds us of the importance of focusing on our purpose during the coming days and not allowing anything to distract us. We must make the most of our time together here in Teotihuacán.

Then, don Miguel begins with his beautiful prayer of gratitude to Father and Mother God. He asks us to close our eyes and listen with our hearts as he explains about our first task of the day, which will be examining and then releasing our attachments.

As I listen to don Miguel's words, I feel a sweet warmth filling my consciousness that allows his words and explanations to go deeper within my consciousness. He begins to explain how our minds are made by emotions. Whatever the mind perceives has an emotional component. Our eyes perceive the light as it is reflected from everything around us. We have a thought about what we perceive, and the thought creates an emotional reaction. Our mind creates a story based on that emotional reaction. This story becomes a part of our dreaming reality. We believe what our mind creates is reality. But this reality is essentially a dream. We dream 24 hours a day, whether the brain is asleep or awake.

The conditioned ways of dreaming our reality have led us into suffering. We suffer because we are afraid of losing what we believe we are and of losing what we have. We are attached to suffering because we believe that it is important to hold onto what we think we are and all the things in our life that reinforce this belief. We hold an image of what we think we should be and judge ourselves according to this image. But our truth is much greater than the image we strive to uphold. We will not understand what we truly are until we let go of that image and our attachment to it. We must let go of the things in our life that have made us feel safe by supporting that image.

We are here in Teotihuacán to create a new dream for our life. Teotihuacán will support us as we travel down the Avenue of the Dead, which is the body of the Feathered Serpent. Today, don Miguel informs everyone that the first task will be for each person to take an inventory of their beliefs and attachments and then release them. We will have a simple ceremony to bury those attachments. Then we will enter the Temple of Quetzalcoatl, which is the first mouth of the two-headed serpent. This will begin the metabolism of our old dream. In a few days, we will emerge from the second mouth, the Pyramid of the Moon. There is much work to do between now and then. Prepare yourselves.

As we begin the first day together with the new group, we walk together and enter the site. I decide my new role will be to participate along with everyone while I help to keep the group together and focused on the task at hand. I know how easy it is to get distracted by these new surroundings. As we enter Teotihuacán and walk toward the Plaza de Quetzalcoatl, there are many things that could distract our new visitors along the way, including the wandering vendors, other tourists, and many new sights and smells all vying for their attention. I now find my previous experience as an elementary school teacher on class field trips to be very helpful for this task.

When we begin today's first task of searching through the Sea of Possibilities for small objects to represent attachments in our life, I take the opportunity to review my attachments once again. I realize that a powerful shift has taken place for me, and now the task feels much lighter. A few days ago, I had to stop and think deeply about the things in my life to which I still felt very attached. I had to carefully examine any remaining threads of attachments. It always seems like there is another loose thread to pull. I know that spiritual growth is like peeling an onion. We remove layer after layer before we reach the core. Something we thought we had let go of and resolved often appears in a slightly different form, and we must face it on another level.

As don Miguel's apprentice, I have been challenging myself for several months to be aware of my relationships and my emotional reactions to everything I experience. Among other challenges, don Miguel had assigned us the task of reviewing our life and creating a mitote book. In essence, don Miguel explains that the concept of mitote is like a big marketplace where many people talk and loudly hawk their wares, but no one is really listening to anyone else. In our mitote book, we have been recording the mitote in our mind. This mitote represents all the inner voices that create confusion and all the emotions that stem from fear. Among our assignments, we were asked to record on a small tape recorder every judgment we made each day and listen to them in the evening. Each of us often had scores of judgements to review each evening—judgements about people and things around us—and, most importantly, judgements about ourselves. That process provided me with a greater understanding of where I've been caught in unhealthy attachments. After all my past experiences, especially including the last few days, I find my task today is much easier, and the attachments are even fewer than I found just a few days ago during my first time here in this plaza.

Now, I also want to support our new companions in each activity. After completing my inventory of some remaining unhelpful beliefs and attachments, I look around to see if others need assistance. I approach some of my new friends individually to check in with them on how it is going. As I do this, I share my experience and help deepen their understanding of the meaning and significance of this task. I explain how we can value, honor, and feel grateful for everything we have been attached to in our life—our home, family, friends, job, status, roles, objects, and everything else. At the same time, we can appreciate the importance of realizing that those things do not make us whole and can even require us to sacrifice our personal freedom in order to keep them in our lives. Henry David Thoreau once said, "We don't ride on the trains, the trains ride on us." This general concept is also true for our possessions, our careers, our mortgages, and often even our relationships.

I remind my new companions that while the Sea of Potential in this plaza represents their life and the joys, attachments, struggles, and challenges they have experienced, it also holds the key to their freedom within it. Hidden within the Sea of Possibilities is a small hologram of the entire site of Teotihuacán. This hologram reflects the ancient Toltec knowledge that every piece of the universe holds the entire universe, just as every human—every being—is a part of the whole that is unique unto itself and yet cannot be separate from all creation.

In order for us to know and understand our higher truth, we must let go of the lies that have made us feel alone and separate. The lies that have kept us tethered to our old, limited beliefs in who we are, as separate beings that need those lies and attachments that we have created to help us feel safe and understand ourselves. It takes a lot of energy to hold together all of these beliefs and attachments. When we free ourselves from them, more energy is available to create our new dream.

If we continue to hold those attachments, we will never allow ourselves to understand who we truly are and the power that we have to create a life of joy, love, and well-being. Today, we are here to begin a process that is one of the most important things we have ever done. Our souls have called us here for this purpose, and don Miguel has provided this gift of vision that has been passed down from his ancient lineage to help show us the path to our truth and reclaim our personal freedom.

The ritual of burying the small objects we have collected today in the dirt of the Island of Safety is but a small gesture. Yet this act can have a great meaning for our lives. In this moment, we have used our personal power and our will to free ourselves from some of the most significant beliefs that have held us back from understanding our own truth and living our life in greater acceptance of that truth.

Although most of us have collected small pebbles or flowers, I notice that one young man is holding a rather large rock. I watch as he slams the rock to the ground, proclaiming loudly that he is tired of carrying that heavy burden any longer!

When we participate in the ceremony of burying our representative objects on the Island of Safety, the act of releasing them opens a new door and pathway to our greater truth. We don't have to stop loving these people and things, but we can allow our love to become completely unconditional. We give them and ourselves the freedom to be held with an open heart and an open hand. When we can let go of our grasping for them, we change our relationship with them, ourselves, and with life.

When we are ready to leave our Island of Safety within the Sea of Possibilities, we climb the steps that lead to the overlook before the Temple of Quetzalcoatl. Here, we imagine jumping into the mouth of the Feathered Serpent. We ceremoniously leave our old life behind and step inside the Temple to meditate and ponder our forthcoming journey through the body of the serpent that offers us the possibility of achieving our personal freedom to live in our own Heaven on Earth. To achieve this amazing potential, we still have many challenges ahead in the coming days.

"The angel of death can be

The greatest teacher we have,

Because death teaches us

To be fully alive."

- don Miguel Ruiz

Black Sun

Chapter XI

From the Angel of Death to the Plaza of Fire

During breakfast the following day, don Miguel informs me that my role today will be the Angel of Death for the new participants. I remember him whispering to me that I am the Angel of Death when he greeted me on my return from the site in the evening two days ago. He tells me that I, as the Angel, will escort each person to him, one by one. There is a field near the hotel with some partially excavated ancient ruins. He tells me that he will be there waiting for us.

Over the past couple of years, I have been intrigued by the Toltec teachings regarding the Angel of Death. We are reminded that we don't own any material things in our life because they all belong to her and will return to her. We each lose many things during our lifetimes, not the least of which are the precious moments that we treasure. When we die, we forfeit every possession, even our own body.

I love to think of the Angel as always having been with me. I imagine her looking over my shoulder and seeing my every experience, observing my every emotional reaction with unconditional love and impartiality. For me, she seems to make each moment even more precious when I pause with awareness, look around me at the people and my surroundings, and realize that I will never see this moment again until I am with her reviewing my life after my physical body has died. I am sincerely grateful for her service, just to know that she is always there, recognized or not, surrounding me with love and her ethereal presence.

I am very honored to accept this role today. After breakfast, we meet as usual in the biblioteca at the hotel. Here, don Miguel explains that, since we have entered the body of the Feathered Serpent by entering the open mouth at the Temple of Quetzalcoatl yesterday, today we will begin our journey down the Avenue of the Dead. He reminds everyone that only the dead are allowed to cross the river near the southern end of the Avenue. If we choose to allow it, the Feathered Serpent will assist us by helping to burn away everything within us that doesn't serve our connection with divinity. So today, we will have a ceremony for passing over into the land of the dead, and then we will prepare for our funeral. This ritual of releasing the old self will help us move forward and create our dream of a new, loving, and joyful life.

This funeral will be a private ceremony that each one will create in their imagination. Each person should make their funeral as real as their imagination can create. It is important to imagine each friend and each family member, to hear what they say, and observe how they act. Only after this is done can we be reborn to our new life and create a new dream in which we can live the rest of our lives in our truth, sharing our love and experiencing our personal freedom. Yesterday, we released and buried old attachments that will not serve us in creating this new life. In our future, we will no longer carry those burdens forward. Without them, we will have greater freedom and energy to create our life anew.

Each person is then instructed to sit quietly in meditation, without speaking to anyone, while they ponder their life, their experiences, and the things they will leave behind as they move forward in building a new dream for their life. As they are meditating, I begin to approach each person, one by one.

After selecting each new person, I first ask them if they are ready for their death. If the answer is yes (and it always was), I take them by the hand and lead them outside the hotel and down the driveway to the entrance to a fenced field where some ancient unrestored ruins can be seen. I lead them to the center of the field, where don Miguel is waiting. He speaks to them and then pretends to chop off their head—symbolically and energetically releasing them from their inner dialog, their constant striving to figure everything out with their mind, unhelpful thoughts, fears, and beliefs. As I start back to retrieve the next person, I notice Trey, Gini, Ted, and Peggy are speaking softly with those waiting for the next step and their rebirth.

The walk from the biblioteca to don Miguel and back takes at least eight to ten minutes. During my walk back with each person, I explain to them how I have always been with them as the Angel of Death. I have been there to witness their experiences, their struggles, and their joys. Even when they felt most alone, the Angel of Death surrounded them with unconditional love and silent encouragement. I'm impressed by many of their reactions as they ponder this thought that the Angel has always been there with them. Most often, they seem ready to play along with our roles. Sometimes, they ask me questions, such as, "Will death hurt?", "How does it feel not to have a body?" or other questions they have been pondering during their time of silent meditation.

This process of retrieving one person at a time provides quite a while for those in the biblioteca to meditate, since there are about thirty people participating. I find it quite lovely to see everyone in quiet meditation. As I walk into the room, which seems to be dimly lit after coming in from the bright sun, I glance around the room at everyone seated and choose the next person with whom I will guide to their "death."

I imagine this is often the way it seems to happen in life. Of all us humans alive in our bodies at any given moment, who will be the next person to die? We never truly know whether we will have another day, decade, or even hour! Eventually, I tap the shoulder of a young woman, who is one of the last to go. When I ask her whether she was ready for her death, "Yes," she whispers in exasperation. "What took you so long?" I smile, wondering how often humans feel that way when their time finally comes.

After everyone has completed their ritual of death, we all walk in silence together toward the site entrance at Puerta 1. From there, we pass through the rows of vendor booths displaying their colorful wares. Again, everyone is reminded to keep their focus and attention on our process for today. Each new participant has only just "died", after all, and now they are heading to prepare for their funerals.

We pass through the visitor center and make a wide left turn when we reach the southern portion of the Avenue of the Dead. As we walk, I point out the small creek representing the river that only the dead can cross. Of course, that is an ancient rule that most other tourists are completely unaware of as they cross the flat bridge over the small creek and continue their exploration of the site.

We soon come to the first set of steps that lead into the Plaza of Earth, or the Plaza of Temptation, as it is also called. After climbing the first set of steps, everyone takes a seat along the steps leading down into the plaza. Ted calls our attention toward the deteriorating Island of Safety in the center of this plaza. It is much smaller than the one we experienced yesterday in the center of the Sea of Possibilities. He reminds everyone how easy and tempting it can be for us to want to hold on to our Island of Safety, to the things we were attached to during our lifetime. But our task here is to bury and release our old selves so that we can create a new, more beautiful dream for our life. All the newly dead are asked to choose a place within the plaza where they will use their imagination to create their own personal burial and funeral ceremony.

Since everyone has been imagining and preparing for this the entire morning, the ceremonies are now completed without delay. After about twenty minutes or so, everyone is ready to be reborn. No one wants to stay "dead" for long!

Together, we make the short trek toward the left side of the plaza, up the steps, and over toward the Place of the Women. Peggy, Gini, and others have brought a few blankets and pillows from the hotel to make the birth process more comfortable. Now, my role becomes a birth doula and/or midwife as each person has the opportunity to "rebirth" themselves. Most of the births are easy, yet also very profound for some individuals as they imagine re-entering the world with new eyes.

Afterwards, I assist in leading each person further into the Women's Temple where the pipe protrudes from the wall within a small nook so each person can take their pretend shower. I'm always amazed at how nice it can feel to imagine the cleansing water flowing down upon you here in this sacred place. Sometimes, I lift the heavy cover to show a new friend the "well" near the shower that supposedly connects energetically to the heaven near the Pyramid of the Moon. In our imaginative vision, this well represents the opening where new souls may emerge to re-enter the physical plane for rebirth here in the Place of the Women.

After their shower, everyone is led to the grassy place under the Pepper trees where don Miguel awaits them. Here, he speaks about what they may experience as a new human being who must begin to create a new way of being in the world. They are now like infants who see life in a new way and must choose to do their best to love, trust, and stay aligned with their highest truth and integrity. Today, they each have the opportunity to begin to create a new, beautiful dream for the rest of their life.

After today's ceremonies, everyone is in high spirits and feeling lighter. We have each left our old lives behind and are ready for what comes next. We take the grassy, cooler path along the west side of the site back to our hotel. It is a warm afternoon, and I decide to go for a swim with some of my new friends in the courtyard pool, where the beautiful fuchsia pink bougainvillea contrasts with the intense turquoise pool.

During the evening gathering, everyone is eager to share their experience of today's rituals for their death, funeral, and rebirth. Yes, it was all an imaginative experience, and yet a physical one as well. We experienced each activity in a physical way that was truly supported by our group and by the physical surroundings here in Teotihuacán.

From this point forward, each of us must choose to experience our life and our world in a more loving and beautiful way. With practice, we will come to understand that our old habits of judging ourselves and others in negative ways no longer feel acceptable. Every moment forward, we must choose between loving or negative, fear-based thoughts. We must pay attention to our emotional reactions and realize whether our thoughts and actions bring us joy or not. If not, we can choose again in the next moment. We must choose now to act with greater integrity. When we choose to see the world through the eyes of love, that love is reflected back to us, and everything around us becomes much more beautiful and alive. This truly is a new beginning if we choose this new dream!

The next day is a whirlwind of activity as we advance northward through the next three plazas along the Avenue of the Dead. We are provided with small red walkie-talkies to facilitate communication and to prevent anyone from getting separated from the group. We use our imagination to allow the Plaza of Water to clean and clear our emotional bodies of old, stagnant emotional energy. We then meditate in the Plaza of Air, focusing on how we have used our breath and our word during our lifetime of experience and how we can choose to use our word in more loving and supportive ways in the future.

Finally, we enter the Plaza of Fire, where the men and women separate to share our thoughts and experiences of what it has meant to be male or female. We reflect on how our early domestication taught us to act and how we came to understand what acceptable or unacceptable behavior was. We consider how this domestication made us feel and how this early training supported or hindered our growth and well-being. After our separate discussions, the men and women reunite in the Plaza of Fire to hug and celebrate the unique qualities that each gender brings. Today, we sincerely respect and acknowledge the beautiful ways yin and yang, male and female, are reflected in the dance of life.

"Beauty is eternity gazing

At itself in the mirror.

But you are eternity

And you are the mirror."

\- Kahlil Gibran

Goddess Rock

Chapter XII

Receiving A Blast from the Heart of Teotihuacán

Gathering on the morning of the fourth day with our new friends, Trey explains the process of recapitulation. He also explains that we will create our "etheric double"—the being we will release when we arrive at the top of the Pyramid of the Moon. He explains the ancient mythology that if we create our etheric double to be a perfect match of our former self with all of the energy of our experiences, beliefs, and attachments, the Eagle will be fooled when he comes to collect us when our body dies. The Eagle will then take our double instead of the "real" us to rejoin the universal energy of consciousness, while the "real" us becomes free to choose our new adventures in spirit. We will replicate this event today by creating and releasing our double on top of the pyramid.

Today, Trey will be leading us in this exercise. The goal of this exercise is to practice opening a channel with Intent in such a powerful way that, through the release of our etheric double, our personal consciousness becomes free to create whatever we choose to experience.

First on today's agenda, we will visit the Plaza of Recapitulation, the fifth and final plaza along the Avenue of the Dead. The exercise of recapitulation of past relationships and events is explained to everyone as a process that helps to free us from habitual emotional reactions that keep us from creating a loving and joyful moment-to-moment experience of life. These habits prevent us from enjoying our personal freedom and connection with our true spirit. Recapitulation is something that historically required months or even years of focus and practice in stalking and retrieving the emotional energy held within old memories, attachments, and beliefs.

While we are here in Teotihuacán, we can connect with the energy of the site to help us with the process. Today, our primary task will be to review our life up to this point, paying particular attention to the events in our life where we experienced upsetting emotional reactions. We are to remember these events with love and forgiveness, release our attachments to them, and reclaim the energy we have previously held in our energy field without awareness. We also return any energy that belongs to others.

In this process, we begin to see how our personal importance has led to suffering. When we revisit our past experiences with love and neutrality, we can see how our personal importance played an important role in how we first viewed the situation. Personal importance leads us to feel sorry for ourselves and to believe that we know better about how things "should" be. We judge others according to this belief. We also judge our body, our abilities, and our experience, and find ourselves lacking. We believe that we know how everyone should act. Our personal importance stems from this knowledge, but we have a distorted understanding of what we truly are and a distorted understanding of "reality".

Certainly, our "reality" is not the same as that of a native person living in the jungle who speaks a very different language. Yet, we judge ourselves and others according to our beliefs that are based on our knowledge. As don Miguel has explained, "It is only knowledge that makes us believe that we are not perfect. Knowledge is nothing more than a description of the dream."

We may even "exile" or compartmentalize parts of ourselves when the part doesn't fit our expectations. It is important to realize that holding on to negative emotions from previous experiences and "exiling" parts of ourselves takes a lot of our personal energy. Now, we must reclaim that energy by remembering, acknowledging, and releasing our emotional hold on these experiences and beliefs. We must understand that past events are in our past; they are not happening now. We must call back the energy that is stuck in old patterns and old beliefs of how things "should" be so that we can allow each moment to shine in its own radiance.

By releasing our attachments to things, beliefs, and experiences, we gain back a lot of personal energy that will help us to create a new, beautiful dream for our life from this moment forward. The past few days here in Teotihuacán have already provided us with many opportunities to free our stuck energy and deeply connect with our true spirit. If we have done the work well, we may discover today that the process of recapitulation in the plaza is easier and that we have less attachment to our past and all the stories we have believed about ourselves.

After our morning gathering, we take our walk to the site in silent meditation. As we walk, we are already beginning our personal recapitulation process. After entering Teotihuacán, we continue walking silently together through each of the four plazas—Earth, Water, Air, and Fire. We focus on the support and teachings that we have received within each of the plazas to help with our recapitulation. Trey reminds us to keep our focus on our personal process as we enter the Plaza of Recapitulation. It is essential to be as thorough as possible in stalking ourselves and honestly examining where we still hold on to old emotional attachments. After we leave this plaza, we will each begin to build our etheric double as we walk toward the Pyramid of the Moon. We will all meet again on the large mesa platform that sits in front of the pyramid.

Upon entering the Plaza of Recapitulation, I decide to remove my shoes in order to feel better connected with the energy of Teotihuacán. As I walk barefoot across the plaza, I begin to focus with gratitude and acceptance for all my life experiences. I acknowledge the gifts that my experiences have provided: the joys and sorrows, the regrets, and the blessings. I feel now that this process of recapitulation gets easier and easier since I've been working on it for months before coming to Teotihuacán.

When I eventually climb the steps at the north end of the plaza, I realize how wonderful I feel and yet how mentally tired I am also feeling. The spiritual and emotional work that we have been focusing on has taken a lot of energy. As I begin my long walk toward the Pyramid of the Moon, I feel like I have very little energy left to concentrate on my task. I want to provide as much focus as possible today for this important mission. I decide to ask Jesus to help me build my etheric double this time. I have been concentrating on my processes so much that my brain definitely needs a little more support. I want to be sure that everything possible is released into my etheric double.

So now, I choose to imagine Jesus walking beside me with every step. This image brings me much comfort. I imagine him helping me pull everything from my energy field that doesn't support my highest truth and connection to my authentic soul and spirit. It seems so much easier with his help. I imagine my etheric double getting larger and larger until it appears to be about twenty feet high. I imagine it wobbling along next to me as it continues to expand like a giant person-shaped helium balloon.

It is a long walk. I feel the solid ground beneath my bare feet and try to walk on the patches of grass along the sides of the avenue as much as I can to avoid the uncomfortable gravel areas. I imagine the energy of the Earth flowing upwards through my foot chakras and the energy of the sun entering through my crown chakra to refresh the depleted energy within my body.

Eventually, I begin to approach the open plaza in front of the Pyramid of the Moon, although the pyramid is still further in the distance. As I walk, my gaze is powerfully drawn toward the large carved rock that I lovingly call the heart of Teotihuacán. As I walk toward the rock, everything else begins to disappear from my vision. I see only the rock, and it feels like I'm being gently pulled toward it. Suddenly, along the horizon of my visual field, I begin to see only dark above the horizon and only white light below the horizon. It reminds me of an aircraft attitude indicator, like the ones I used to test when I worked for the US Air Force. Of course, a pilot would only see the instrument in this orientation when the plane is flying upside-down!

I gaze intently toward this horizon as I continue to be propelled forward toward the rock. Suddenly, all along the horizon, I see a thin line of bright orange-yellow flames appearing. The fires begin to expand and grow along the horizon line. After a while, the flames separate into several balls of flame. I watch them grow into large, round fires, at least four or five of them. As soon as this happens, all the separate flaming spheres merge into a single bright ball that immediately transforms into a ball of pure black light energy. Now, in a powerful blast, this black ball of energy zooms toward me and hits me in the center of my forehead. The blast is so strong that I am physically thrown backwards in the air at least five or six feet.

I am shocked to find myself lying on my back on the ground. That was definitely amazing—whatever that was! I realize I'm not hurt at all because I landed safely on the cushion of my backpack. I see that I am now just about twenty feet in front of the wonderful rock. My friend Peggy rushes over to help me up. I assure her I'm fine and try to explain what had happened, at least what I had seen happening. She begins to walk with me, her arm around me for support. Peggy's husband, Ted, also comes over because he has also seen what happened, or at least the result of it, from his point of view. I try to explain what I had experienced to him, as well.

Ted tells me that I should not go up onto the Pyramid of the Moon because it would be dangerous if it happened again and I was thrown off the pyramid. I try to tell him that I'm fine. I know that the whole thing was something generated by the powerful rock and my attraction to it, so I'm sure it wouldn't happen on the Pyramid. Ted still insists that I shouldn't go up onto the Pyramid. But I don't believe there's any reason I shouldn't go. To resolve our minor standoff, Ted decides that Trey should make the decision since he will be leading the group ceremony up on the pyramid.

Ted leads me over to Trey and tells him that it could be dangerous for me to climb the Pyramid since I had just flown backwards several feet without an apparent explanation. I explain what I think just happened. Trey takes one look at me and says, "You don't need to go up on the Pyramid because you have just released your etheric double already!" After hearing Trey's pronouncement, I reluctantly agree to stay behind.

I climb up onto the mesa platform in front of the pyramid to wait for the group. I think to myself that at least it will be nice to have a little rest here. My friend Katherine is already there, sitting on a blanket. She motions for me to share her blanket. From where we sit, we can watch our group climbing up the stairs of the Pyramid. There are many tourists also climbing on the Pyramid, but I know what some of the people in our group are wearing, so I can pick them out from the other tourists, even though everyone is far enough away that they appear to be about the size of ants.

After our group reaches the top of the pyramid, I am still able to see them because I can tell they are standing together as a large group, mostly in the center area. When the ceremony begins, I am amazed to be able to hear Trey's voice. This surprises me very much! Why is it that I can hear him when I can barely see our group at all from this distance?

I think Trey has probably been speaking for a few minutes before I realize that I am hearing him speaking, because there is a lot of background noise all around us due to the other tourists. So, when I start to listen closely, I hear Trey talking about the black sun. This is the black light that the ancient Toltecs referred to as the source of the physical sun, which, in turn, provides the energy that manifests all life on Earth. It is also the same black light that had jolted me into the air just a few minutes ago.

I hear Trey instructing the group to look up at the sun above their heads. I look up and realize that the high clouds today obscure enough of the sunlight that it doesn't hurt my eyes to look at it, although the sun is clearly visible as a sphere of light. Now, I can clearly hear Trey saying, "See the black sun spiraling around the yellow sun. The black sun is now at the top of the sun, now it is at the bottom, now it's back at the top."

I look up and watch a small black orb moving around the yellow sun, and I see that it is always in the position Trey describes. Wow! Not only can I hear Trey's voice right now, but I am also amazed to actually see the black sun as it spirals around our visible sun. How can this be? I ask Katherine whether she can hear Trey's voice. She is sitting a couple of feet away from me. She replies that she isn't sure whether or not she can hear him.

As the short ceremony ends, I see everyone on the top of the pyramid raise their arms to the sky as they release their etheric double. A faint cheer also seems to come from them. At this point, some of our group start their descent and begin walking back down the Pyramid steps. Others stay a while, enjoying the view of Teotihuacán and the entire valley all the way to the surrounding mountains.

It isn't until a short while later, when I open my backpack to get a drink of water, that I realize the reason I had been able to hear Trey's voice is right in there. I have completely forgotten that the small red walkie-talkie is still in my backpack! Apparently, when I landed on my back after the black light hit my forehead, the jolt must have turned it on! So that is a simple explanation for one "miracle" today. But the miracle of seeing the black sun as it spirals around our physical sun and the miracle of getting hit in the forehead by a powerful blast of black light that sent me flying backwards will probably go unanswered (at least in terms of normal physical reality) for the rest of my natural life.

What a beautiful, amazing, miraculous day this has been. We head back to the hotel and then over to the nearby family restaurant for a wonderful dinner. While I am eating, I tell Trey about the "miracle" of hearing his voice even though he was far away and how I saw the black sun spiraling around the yellow sun just the way he had described. Trey then offers to let me use the headphones connected to his portable CD player. He wants me to listen to the words in the David Bowie song called "Changes" because the lyrics reflect in interesting ways what we are experiencing as we transform our lives here on this Teotihuacán power journey. "Ch-ch-ch-changes!"

"The entire reason for being on Earth

Is to Love.

Love is God, and God is Love.

Nothing matters but Love."

- Houston Asher

In his eulogy for his friend John Paul

Pyramid of the sun

Chapter XIII
The Final Ceremony

Today is the final full day of our time here in Teotihuacán. Everyone is in high spirits at breakfast and feeling very connected with everyone here in our group. We have all shared many powerful experiences together during the past few days. Even though most of us did not know one another before this week, we have grown close. We know that the training and practice that we have received will certainly make a difference for the rest of our lives. We have received many wonderful gifts of awareness and transformation from don Miguel, Trey, and all the other teachers who are passing on this legacy.

Teotihuacán has provided a wonderful map and guidance for our spiritual growth. I have often experienced profound inspirations and messages that seem to be offered by the site itself and/or through the consciousness of the ancient ones who wish to share the powerful knowledge with those who are open and willing to hear and see the messages. Several times, don Miguel has mentioned that "Teotihuacán is awakening". I feel this aliveness here. Could this awakening provide humanity a path to discovering our true divine nature again after millennia of something akin to dormancy? My experiences here certainly make me think so! Of course, our divine nature has never been dormant; it is only our conscious awareness of it that could be described as dormant. Perhaps humanity is slowly awakening (in fits and starts) to a greater understanding of consciousness and what is possible for us to experience.

As always, I have been very impressed with the generous way that don Miguel treats everyone. Each person is treated with loving respect, whether someone is new to the teaching or a long-time apprentice. Don Miguel insisted that we treat one another with respect, as well. I have only known him to be impeccable in respecting everyone. I have seen don Miguel make an effort to connect with each person individually and give them a warm hug, especially those new to the group. Many times, I have experienced an atmosphere where, in simple words, everyone feels a deeply loving connection with everyone around them. We have an agreement never to gossip and to be respectful to each other and everyone around us. This atmosphere of love and respect feels so seamless to me that we hardly notice how amazing it is to feel and act with such harmony and love for others in such a large group for days and days. But it is pretty amazing!

This morning, everyone is excitedly anticipating our final ceremony, to be held on top of the Pyramid of the Sun. During the morning meeting, don Miguel tells us that we will each will have a partner for our walk in silence to the site entrance. We must be careful not to speak with our partner or anyone. Although I didn't fully understand the importance of this rule at the time, I have come to believe that don Miguel was often using silence as a tool for developing personal discipline, among other purposes. I realize now that this is because, to progress along the Toltec path, one must have a high degree of personal discipline. Personal discipline has always been an important consideration for Toltec masters and their apprentices, as much as it has been for many other spiritual and martial arts training throughout human history.

As students, we can hear the teachings and think we understand them, but actually living them when we return home is the true challenge, and that takes discipline! Mostly, self-discipline is important to develop because it is very easy to carry on with old habits that have been a part of our lives since childhood.

Today is a beautiful, warm January morning with just a few high clouds as we gather outside the hotel. Everyone is provided with a walking partner. My partner today is Steven. As the group begins walking behind don Miguel, I see that he is leading us along the right side of the site. As a group, we have not previously gone this way, but I remember that this is the way that I returned alone as the sun was setting on the last day of the first session. That was the wonderful evening when I found the dog carcass and then don Miguel had christened me as the Angel of Death.

At the beginning of our walk, Steven and I start off holding hands. However, our path is quite long, and since Steven is very tall but I am not, we eventually let go and continue walking side by side. We are probably at about the halfway point when I happen to glance up at the sky. There in the sky, I notice a long, narrow cloud directly above me. For some reason, I think to myself that the cloud looks like the arm of God reaching across the sky.

It reminds me a little of the painting by Michelangelo on the ceiling of the Sistine Chapel, where God reaches down to touch Adam's outstretched hand. My eyes follow along the length of the arm cloud through the sky to look for the hand. However, I don't see a hand with an outstretched finger reaching down as it appears in the painting. I wonder why that is. But soon, I realize that instead of God's finger serenely pointing downward as it does in the painting, the hand is cupped and seems to hold something. I try to make out what it holds. To my amazement, I realize that the shape of the cloud looks exactly as if an angel is sitting in the cupped hand of God. I see the body of the angel, and there is the head and the wings. How amazing is it to distinctly see an arm of God spanning across the sky with its hand clearly holding an angel!

Steven and I continue walking silently along the path next to the site's perimeter fence. After a few more minutes, I look up into the sky again, wondering how the clouds might have moved due to the wind in the atmosphere. In my experience, clouds usually move and change their shape every few minutes. But this cloud formation looks exactly the same as it appeared before. Every time I look up after walking a few more minutes along the path, I see that the cloud stays exactly as it appeared when I had first noticed it. It seems quite remarkable to me that it isn't changing at all.

Eventually, a thought comes to me that I could be that angel sitting in the hand of God, looking down at myself walking along the path. For a while, I play with that image. I imagine myself up there looking down at me. Then I change my point of view to back down here looking up, also at myself. How wonderful it all appears as I play with my point of view—my point of perception—going back and forth.

Soon, I decide to imagine what I would be seeing if I were actually up there looking down, not just at myself, but also at the entire site of Teotihuacán. I imagine seeing it from the air, looking down at the Avenue of the Dead. I see the Pyramids and every part of the site. It all seems very clear and real in my mind's eye. I can really see (and imagine) the whole site as I would see it if I were looking down from high above!

Playfully passing time this way, it isn't long before we reach the entrance to the parking lot for Puerto 4, the Sun Gate. Don Miguel is standing near the fence at the driveway entrance to the parking lot. At the exact moment that he hands me a ticket to the site, my consciousness suddenly shifts dramatically. I really can't put into words how different everything around me appears. The best I can say is that I feel almost like I am floating as I move across the gravel parking lot. I'm not sure where Steven is right now, but I see a few others in our group walking toward some trees and a few vendor booths at the other side of the parking lot, so I decide to go that way.

Suddenly, I am aware of a man hysterically and joyfully laughing somewhere behind me. I am absolutely drawn toward that wonderful sound! It seems that sound reflects exactly the way that I am feeling right now, and I really want to be near whoever it is. I look over my left shoulder to see where the laughter is coming from and who it might be. I see three men from our group walking together. Ted is on one side, and Trey is on the other. Between them, I see Fu-Ding, who is being supported, almost carried along by Ted and Trey. It's as if Fu-Ding is having trouble walking, or maybe Ted and

Trey are trying to guide him in the right direction because it's obvious that Fu-Ding is oblivious to everything around him.

I move closer to the three of them and continue walking toward the entrance. I feel like I am almost exactly in the same emotional state as Fu-Ding, but I don't need anyone to carry me. Suddenly, I'm aware that another woman from our group is approaching the trio. She worriedly says, "Don't let his wife Linda see him like this. It will really upset her." I don't yet know Linda and Fu-Ding well, but I think that I would be very happy if my husband were laughing like that! At this moment, I can't imagine why Linda, or any wife, would be upset.

I notice that most of our group is waiting for others by the restroom near the entrance. I stop briefly there and then move forward until I approach the steps into the museum. I notice a woman who I think must be Linda, Fu-Ding's wife. She stands near the top of the steps, looking back toward where I last heard Fu-Ding. She has a very worried expression.

Somehow, Linda's expression affects me in a strange way. I lose my momentum and have to almost force myself to ascend the steps. I eventually make it to the top step, but no further. I am somewhat aware of our group going inside the museum, but I'm quite unable to move. I stand there suspended for some time. Eventually, I notice two large, narrow plaques on each side of the entrance. The plaques are about eight feet high and a couple of feet across. They have much information on them in Spanish. I haven't really studied Spanish since grade school, when I learned just a little. But now, I'm amazed that I can read the detailed information on the signs. They explain the history and geology of the site of Teotihuacán and the valley in which it is situated. I have no idea why I can suddenly read Spanish so well.

After being stuck near the entrance for what seems like 20 minutes or more, I am suddenly concerned that I don't know where anyone in our group has gone or whether I will be able to find them. I must will myself to move, so I will myself to step inside. Once inside, I look around, but don't see anyone I know at first. After a while, I recognize don Miguel standing far back down

145

a museum hallway. I move toward him, feeling like I'm being pulled toward him by some kind of magnetism. I'm hoping he doesn't move away since I'm not sure how I would find him again.

But don Miguel doesn't move away, and I'm soon next to him. He turns toward me and says, "Go gather everyone and have them come to this room." As he says this, he motions toward a bright nearby room with an open doorway. I wonder whether I could possibly find anyone right now. He then looks at me again, immediately sees the state I'm in, and says, "Oh, never mind." Then he takes my hand and leads me into the room.

As I step into the room, my mind is "blown" because just below my feet, under a transparent glass floor, I see the entire site of Teotihuacán, just as I had been seeing it while I was walking and imagining that I was the angel sitting in the hand of God! At first, I am almost frightened and squeeze don Miguel's hand until I realize that I can actually walk on the clear glass floor and not fall from the sky! He then brings me over to where Gloria, another woman from our group, is standing. She is holding on to a horizontal metal bar or pipe railing near the side of the room. Currently, my altered consciousness doesn't quite take in everything around me, but the bar looks quite solid and safe. Don Miguel puts my hand on the bar and says, "Hold on to this and stay here."

I gladly take hold of the bar. This seems like the only thing I can do right now. Soon, the rest of our group is gathered in the room around the edges of the three-dimensional site map. I can hear don Miguel speaking to them about the site. It's hard for me to understand his words. My capacity for the meaning of words seems quite limited right now. But I feel the meaning going into my consciousness at a deep, non-verbal level.

Although I have trouble understanding the words he says, I am getting parts of it in a more profound way than I have ever experienced. It's a little distorted now as I attempt to explain it in words, but I will try. The most important thing I comprehend from his talk is that when Teotihuacán was designed, it was physically built to honor the beautiful dance between male and female energy, between the yin and the yang. Everyone is gathered around the sides of the three-dimensional model of the site that is under the glass floor, as don Miguel points out aspects of the site. He speaks about the Pyramid of the Sun representing the male energy—action, light, physical strength, narrow focus, decisiveness, and analytical knowledge. Then he explains how the Pyramid of the Moon represents the female energy—nurturing, wide focus, creativity, the void—that dark place where creation begins, introspective, and the silent knowing of intuition. Even though the Pyramid of the Sun is larger than the Pyramid of the Moon, they were originally built to reach the same height because the ground slopes upward as you move from the Sun Pyramid to the Moon Pyramid. Together, these two energies are necessary for the creation of physical life. They are meant to naturally respect and support each other in a beautiful dance of balance and harmony. He seems to explain how each of these energies longs for the other in a deep way that propels them together to facilitate this true balance, harmony, and creation. It's hard now to explain in words what I'm experiencing. I feel many concepts and images that don Miguel is imparting wash over me with such a profound depth that it seems as if my mind is only capturing just a whiff or an aroma of them—as if there is so much more that is crossing the threshold in another level of my consciousness than my mind can grasp.

After don Miguel speaks, he tells everyone to follow him outside the room. They leave through a door in the back of the room. I am still securely holding on to the bar. As they leave, I am suddenly struck by a profound longing for the masculine. I have never felt this way before. I feel a sweet, almost melancholy desire for the masculine wash over me. Just at this moment, I look up from where I am standing toward an area behind the bar that supports me. Right before my eyes, I suddenly notice a huge floor-to-ceiling window! Just a few yards on the other side of the window, I see the enormous Pyramid of the Sun. The entire pyramid is intensely illuminated by the morning sunlight. At this moment, it seems to be the most beautiful sight I have ever seen! My sudden longing for the masculine is reflected powerfully by the sunlight on the Pyramid. The sight is almost overwhelmingly beautiful to me now. I wonder how it can be possible for me to have been standing right here for all this time and not even seeing what has always been right in front of me? And it's so beautiful! I feel so drawn to it.

It's not long before Trey and another man come back to help Gloria and I to come join the group. I think Gloria starts walking toward them, but I can't seem to let go of the bar yet. So, Trey comes over and guides me by the shoulders as we walk toward the door. He places his hands over my eyes as we walk outside the room and guides me forward. It seems like we pass several museum exhibits until we reach a place where I can feel a wall near my left arm. Trey carefully positions me and then removes his hands from over my eyes. Before me now, I see a bright and beautiful ancient alabaster sculpture on the display shelf in front of my eyes that somehow appears to represent the sun! The beauty and masculine power of the sculpture overwhelms me so much by its intense brightness that I start to fall backwards. Thankfully, Trey is still behind me and catches me before I fall. Trey asks me if I'm all right, and I reply, "Yes, that piece is just so beautiful that I was surprised!"

I want to stay for a while by the sculpture, but Trey then guides me out the back door of the museum, where don Miguel and the group are waiting. Another friend, Linda Lightfoot, notices me and rushes over to give me a hug. But before she reaches me, don Miguel steps in and stops her. He then guides me over to Steven and tells me to hug him. When I do, Steven almost immediately collapses to the ground, sobbing. I realize that he must have felt some kind of powerful charge that I couldn't explain—but it must have come from somewhere beyond me!

After that, I feel almost back to my normal consciousness as don Miguel begins to lead the group toward the steps of the Pyramid of the Sun. Once again, I begin to climb according to the ancient ceremonial way, and at each of the three level areas, I walk counterclockwise at the edge of the Pyramid while the men walk clockwise.

When we all reach the top of the Pyramid, we gather and begin our meditation guided by don Miguel. His words seem to help me to create my personal channel to the sun. I find the connection so powerful that my consciousness seems to disappear into a beautiful channel of intensely bright energy that flows from the center of the Earth to the center of the Sun and back again. For a while, I completely melt into that channel. There is nothing but intense light everywhere around me. After a while, I begin to hear someone speaking. Don Miguel is offering a prayer of gratitude to Heaven and Earth for all we are experiencing here. We complete the ceremony in a group hug. I have never felt such a beautiful unity with others, and we remain together in this way for a long time.

Eventually, it is time to descend. I look around and see that don Miguel is already gone. As we gather our backpacks, hats, and water bottles, I notice a Mexican woman approaching Steven. I hear her telling him in English that, although she is Catholic, she feels that our group embodies God's energy in a beautiful and respectful way. He nods and thanks her.

I walk back down the steps of the Pyramid with a few friends, singing softly with open hearts as we go. I decide to visit what I call the Heart Rock and then take my friends along to show them the Palace of the Butterflies (the place don Miguel calls Heaven), the rooms of the ancient priests, and the Portal. I am so happy to connect with these places one last time before I leave Teotihuacán.

We decide to leave the site through the closest exit, Puerta 3, or the Moon Gate. Along the way out, there are shops where we buy a few souvenirs and gifts for our friends and family. I find a small mosaic figure of the head of Quetzalcoatl made of broken turquoise pieces and a small, green glass and obsidian replica of the Pyramid of the Sun to bring home. I am happy to find a couple of gifts for my daughters. I also purchase a terra cotta figure of the Aztec god of fire, Xiuhtecuhtli.

It's a long walk back to the hotel, but we are happy and enjoy the beauty of the pepper trees and the beautiful high desert vegetation along the way. Back in my room, I enjoy a warm shower before we gather for our last meeting together.

Before dinner, we meet in the biblioteca for our final meeting. I feel surrounded by a warm, almost buzzing, sense of lightness, connection, and gratitude for all we have experienced over the past few days. Everyone in the group seems tired but deeply joyful.

Don Miguel begins our meeting by reminding us that each of us has come to Teotihuacán because we knew there was more to life than what we had experienced. He explains that the most important thing we have been doing here is beginning to create a new dream for our lives—a dream based on unconditional love. We have been practicing that new dream every day since we arrived. We must continue to practice in order to master our new dream.

All our life, we have been creating a dream, and we have already mastered that old dream. That dream was based on what we believed. It was based on what we were taught about who we are, how to behave, what is acceptable, and what is not acceptable. It was based on knowledge. Knowledge is not good or bad. It is essential to our physical survival and for communicating with our fellow humans. But most of what we have learned is not exactly true. It is only true from a certain point of view. We have believed that we know who we are, but that was from the point of view of knowledge. We have created a whole story of our life that comes from knowledge. We believe that we are the main characters of our story.

But in truth, we are Life! Life is the force that moves our body. It is the same force that moves every human body. It is the same force that moves the stars, and it is undefinable. Our imagination can understand what we really are, but there are no words to explain what we are. In our imagination, we can shift our point of view from knowledge to life. This is an act of power.

"I hope", says don Miguel, "that you had a glimpse of your truth during our ceremony on top of the Pyramid of the Sun today. In that moment, you can see who you really are. Once you have this experience, you can always remember."

In the past, we created a story about our lives based on knowledge. We don't have to fight against knowledge. But with Awareness, we can realize that we have been trapped in that story, even though it was never who we are. When we were born, we did not have knowledge. We came into this life completely innocent, but with unconditional love.

There is a story in the Bible about when the Savior came into the world, and the beast was waiting to devour the Savior. Of course, this is a metaphor. We can say that the beast is actually our culture with many beliefs, rules, and superstitions that are based on fear. We can call the beast "The Devil" or "The Dream of the Planet". The beast has many names and grows stronger within us when we feed it our fear. We may not even recognize our fear when it is masked as anger, sadness, frustration, anxiety, shame, or helplessness.

In a way, we can say that this beast has been feeding on our personal energy and depriving us of our personal freedom. We are not free when we are not living according to our highest truth because we choose to conform out of fear to rules that do not serve us.

In our life, the savior must be us. Even if we choose to acknowledge Christ, Buddha, Muhammad, or another as our savior, still, only we can decide whether we want to live according to outside rules that are mostly based on lies and fear. Our authentic savior understands what serves our truth and knows that the choice must come from within us. This has always been true. It requires courage to take action guided by the source within our heart. We can begin to save ourselves by choosing a new joyful and loving dream.

We didn't choose all the knowledge we learned. But as we saw in the Plaza of Quetzalcoatl—the Plaza of Hell—our knowledge makes us feel comfortable and safe. That's okay—it's perfect and the Island of Security is our impressive creation. Now, here in Teotihuacán, it is evident that we are not what we have believed. The challenge will be to decide whether we want to return to our old story where we felt comfortable and safe, or choose to create a new dream to live in a loving relationship with integrity and life.

When we go home, we know that everyone around us will tell us what they believe. They will expect us to agree with them. They will not be pleased if we try to convince them otherwise. They need us to agree with them to feel safe. When our beliefs are not based in truth, we need others to agree and validate those beliefs. Social agreement is the only way to sustain beliefs that are not exactly true. We do not have to believe those around us, but if we listen, they will tell us how they dream. If we hear something that resonates with our truth, we can use it to grow our personal dream. If it doesn't resonate, we can let it go with respect.

When we know that we come from unconditional love, we do not need to judge anyone. They are perfect the way they are. We can respect their dream because we understand it, and we have dreamed in that way before. But we must not give away our personal freedom by choosing to live in their drama. Unconditional love does not create drama.

When we live from the point of view of Life, everything becomes easy. We simply take the action that we need to take. We can choose to be our own hero or heroine. We will be kind to our physical body and choose our emotional reactions so that our bodies receive healthy, loving hormones rather than stressful and harmful ones. We can respect ourselves enough never to go against ourselves.

There will be false prophets. They will try to convince us of their superstitions. When we return home, we will have to choose whether to believe those who say they have the answers. They can only take someone to the place where they are, according to their beliefs and superstitions. Life in a human body is short. We must decide whether we want to live according to those superstitions or not.

We can be our own masters and teachers. We must not take our own freedom away. We must value the freedom to be what we are, whatever we are, without needing to justify or define ourselves to anyone. In Teotihuacán, we have had a taste of our truth. Now, it is up to us to create a new dream based on our own truth.

"The only way to master love

Is to practice love.

You don't need to justify your love,

You don't need to explain your love;

You just need to practice your love.

Practice makes the master."

\- don Miguel Ruiz

Ceremony on top of the pyramid of the sun

Chapter XIV
Homeward Bound

I awaken on this final morning in Teotihuacán once again filled with gratitude. I know that there will be many challenges to face when I return home. I feel like a completely transformed human. In a way, I feel like I have shed a thousand beliefs and a thousand weights while I have been here. I have shed beliefs that existed in an old dream that was never real. This morning, I have so much compassion for my human and all her struggles within that dream. There were always so many concerns and so many balls to keep in the air—between home, family, and work—and especially maintaining the image that I wanted to present to the world. It took a lot of energy to keep everything together and in some kind of order. I have no idea how I will be able to re-enter my life and integrate my new understandings. I know I will have to continue to support my family and keep up with all my projects at work. But now, all of that will have to wait for another day.

Today, I choose to trust in Spirit and Intent. As don Miguel has reminded us, "Intent has nothing to do with the mind." I will align with Intent. The image of Intent in the form of Tezcatlipoca on the Temple of Quetzalcoatl has permeated my consciousness in a very profound way. The two circles that appear in the figure on the side of the temple seem to open my consciousness like a doorway into the infinite that reveals the dark void of creation. Somehow, I feel very aligned with that doorway—that feeling of expansion and expansiveness. It seems to touch the core of my being, offering profound peace and acceptance. It imparts a sense of boundless infinity, yet it also seems to hold a great mystery that I deeply desire to explore. Oh, my words cannot do it justice!

This morning, as I repack my suitcase, I have the feeling that I will be stepping into a completely unknown territory. As I walked barefoot through Teotihuacán, the energy of the grounds permeated my body. This place and this hotel have become familiar territory, while the future is not. I know that so much of this place and my experiences here will come with me, although the attachment feels light and effortless. It is time now to go on my way, even though Teotihuacán will always be my home. A home for my heart.

As the bus leaves the hotel driveway on our way to the airport in Mexico City, I sit in an aisle seat near the front, where I have a good view of the road and the southern boundary of Teotihuacán on my right. After we clear the entry roundabout and move out onto the highway, I am surprised to feel a powerful, physical tug at my solar plexus and all my internal organs. It feels something like a big rubber band connecting me with Teotihuacán and threatens to pull me back there. I try to examine this energy, to see what it is about. What I see in my mind's eye are some nonphysical, feminine beings that are connected with Teotihuacán from ancient times. I tell them I am grateful for their guidance, care, and connection, and that I will definitely return. This promise seems to lessen the tug a bit.

At the airport, I am pleased to learn that quite a few of my new friends will be on the same flight that I have booked, at least the first leg from Mexico City to Phoenix. We have a fairly early flight, so our wait at the airport is rather short. Somehow, with all I have to carry and keep track of as I negotiate my way through the airport, I end up leaving behind the small figure of Xiuhtecuhtli, the Aztec god of fire. I was drawn to him primarily because I love the concept of fire and its cleansing powers, but he is an Aztec figure, not Toltec. Since I have no idea about the mythology concerning him, I decide it's a minor loss.

When it comes time to board the flight, I am surprised that one of the stewardesses greets each passenger personally and asks where they have been and how long we stayed. She is very cordial and friendly. This is still January 1997, so the rules on the plane are very pleasant and open. During the three-hour flight, we often leave our seats to chat with one another, share many stories with lots of laughter, and we have a great time. No one seems to care if we stand in the aisle and lean into a friend's seat.

Whenever I am in my own seat for takeoff and landing, I find myself drawn into the blue fabric of the seat in front of me because it is a beautiful, dark blue color with rows of stars. I repeat to myself, "I am the space between the stars…" I look outside my window and down at the clouds below. I am amazed to see a perfect shadow of our plane on the clouds below with a beautiful, circular rainbow surrounding the shadow of the plane. I feel surrounded by protection, and I am enjoying the experience of seeing miracles all around!

After the plane lands and we begin to get off, that cordial stewardess keeps asking us, "Where did you say you have been? And what did you do???" She seems pretty impressed, as if she has never seen a group as joyful as ours! At the airport terminal in Phoenix, I keep noticing the dark blue carpets because they seem to be covered with stars and circles that remind me of the eyes of Intent, just as the back of the seats on the airplane had. Images of birds also appear in the carpet. These images remind me of the mythology of the phoenix bird, which rose from the ashes and flew into the heavens. It's a very appropriate image for us today, I think. I do find it challenging to simply find my way through the airport. I must keep my full attention on every step I take. Just navigating through the airport here in the physical world seems disorienting to me. I feel very energetically open, so much that the buzzing energy of each person around me makes it quite hard to look at anyone. I decide to implement a circle of protection around my body, and I imagine a row of white roses along the edge of that circle. This helps quite a bit. The roses provide an energetic barrier that helps define and separate my own energetic space from the energy of the people around me.

When I arrive back in Sacramento, Betty is there to meet me at the airport and bring me back to her house so I can retrieve my car. I am very grateful for her assistance, as I'm unsure whether I could navigate to her house without help. Normally, of course, I could easily get there on my own, but I'm not yet in my usual frame of consciousness. I still feel very open, and it's difficult to focus. It's an amazing feeling that I'm not yet ready to relinquish.

When we arrive at her home, Betty and I have a wonderful time catching up and sharing our stories of Teotihuacán. My consciousness is still very expanded, so much so that everything around me feels very different than it did when I was last here, eleven days ago. Before I go, I ask her if I can use her restroom. When I walk in, I notice a clock on the shelf. For some reason, I find that incredibly funny! I can't help laughing at why humans would ever feel it is necessary to know what time it is, even in the restroom. What a crazy dream humans have created! I don't think it's anything personal about Betty. She didn't create this dream; she just has to live in it.

It is getting dark when I put my suitcase in the car and get in. Even though it's been only eleven days since I drove my car and parked it here, it feels so strange now that I can hardly remember what I am supposed to do. "What is this thing I'm in? What controls am I supposed to touch and engage? Where should I put my hands now?" I realize that I can only shift into autopilot. I must trust in Spirit and align with Intent. There is no other way that I can perform this action now using my cognitive mind and reason. So, I shift into that mode and find that driving my car home now is very easy. That shift makes it possible for me to take the action that I need to take. I imagine that this will be the way I can function from this moment forward.

"This place is a dream.

Only a sleeper thinks it's real.

Then death comes like a dawn.

And you wake up laughing

At what you thought was your grief."

- Rumi

Chapter XV
Practice Into Action

My first journey to Teotihuacán was powerful, magical, and very challenging. I have been forever grateful for this life-changing experience. It was everything and so much more than I had dreamed it would be. In writing this book, it has been very exciting to realize how alive and present these experiences remain for me, even today, when I align with the moment and the emotions I felt then. Emotions are truly a powerful gateway to memory. Even though I have been unable to locate the journal I kept during this trip, I have been fascinated by how time seemed to become flexible and fold back upon itself to reveal how unreal our illusions of linear time must be. It is so easy for humans to think that precious moments in our past are lost to us, except through fuzzy memories and faded photographs.

In fact, the precious moments of our life are never lost to us. From a certain point of view, we can say that the angel of death witnesses them and holds them for us—she is our mirror. We always have access to the spacious present, which is this moment. Like a hologram, this moment holds everything we have ever experienced. The key is where we choose to place our attention. When we release our attachment to that which has caused suffering, we free our attention for more rewarding and productive pursuits. From that point of perception, we allow ourselves to be open to new experiences and abilities that we never thought possible. My experiences in Teotihuacán undeniably revealed this again and again.

I have learned so much to appreciate that we are multidimensional beings who truly have access to time and space in ways that we can only imagine. We can share, learn, love, and experience so much more on so many "levels" of creation and experience than we may now understand. Our consciousness is not limited by what we think we know. I love the quote by Thoreau that says, "Man's capacities have never been measured. Nor are we to judge what he can do by precedents, so little has been tried."

When I practice the process of recapitulation, as I did in Teotihuacán and for months prior to going, I realized how powerful it can be to reclaim energy that I left in past experiences, even many years later. This energy became available for me to use in creating my experience of life in powerful and ever more beautiful ways. I no longer have to hold onto painful experiences and have my energy trapped in past events that never served me. I know that my personal freedom to choose is always in the present moment; it is only now in this moment that I can create anew.

I want to share with you something that I wrote shortly after I returned from Teotihuacán:

Reflections on Teotihuacán 01/28/97

From my perspective today, one of the most exciting things about my experience in Teo is the way things synchronized totally. The magic of my inner dream, including many inner experiences that happened over the past several years (even going back to my childhood), were expressed or mirrored outside in things that I had before considered to be external to myself. There was a continual and amazing validation of my inner visions by external events that occurred. The things I desired most would appear, as if by magic! Things I had seen in the sky would appear before my feet. When the dog skeleton on the ground told me that the Angel of Death was near, a short time later, I was asked to become her "officially" for the day. But then, this angel has always been close to my heart.

In terms of everyday Reason, there were far too many profound coincidences to ignore. It was impossible to write them all down in my journal; they happened almost continuously. There was a complete merging of my inner and outer dream, and the results were pure joy and immense gratitude. If my Reason ever wants to argue that this is impossible, I'm sure it could try, but my heart and all my being know it is true and that it all happened as clearly as anything else I've ever experienced in my life. If magic can be true for ten days of my life, it can certainly be true for always.

How wonderful my life will be from now on! All that I must do is remember to surrender to the Temple—the Temple that exists in Teo and everywhere. (At least, this is how it worked in Teo!) I must honor my Spirit by surrendering my Reason, by looking for the magic, and taking action when it calls to me. These are my highest aspirations now. I know that I must keep my awareness and stalk the magic at every moment. In this way, life will always hold its charm. I have found that I can unconditionally trust Spirit to provide all that I need and far more! I don't need to go against myself any longer. I can totally honor the God of my Heart, knowing that what I most need and desire will be provided. This is the lasting gift of Teotihuacán.

* * * * *

An interesting thing happened a couple of months after my Teotihuacán journey. In late March, we gathered in Santa Fe with don Miguel to celebrate Easter. At this event, don Miguel surprised me by fastening a watch made of gummy candy on my wrist. It had a wide band and was green with some pink swirls in the candy. As he fastened it, he stated, "Now you will always know what time it is!" I wore it for a couple of days until it began to sort of melt.

I always wondered why he gave me that gummy watch. He usually had a reason for his actions, but I wasn't sure what this was about. It wasn't the kind of thing I had known him to do, and he didn't give one to anyone else, as far as I knew.

However, as I was writing this story, I laughed when I finally realized what may have been his reason for presenting me with the watch. When I wrote about my experience in Betty's bathroom after returning to Sacramento, I tried to explain how amusing it was to me in that moment to think about how humans in our culture always want to know what time it is—even in the bathroom! Perhaps the gift of the watch was don Miguel's way of letting me know that he had heard my musings that day. It certainly wasn't unusual for him at that time to be aware of how I and other apprentices were feeling and incorporating his teachings during the weeks between our sessions. He would always amaze me with his astute observations of what our struggles and successes had been when we were apart. To each one of us, it always seemed like he was talking about exactly what we had personally been experiencing.

What an amazing and sweet connection he constantly revealed to me during the years of my apprenticeship. I had to acknowledge over and over to myself that, as spiritual beings, we are never actually alone. We share a connection as life and as one being, even when we forget who we truly are.

As I look back on those early years of my apprenticeship from this point in my life, I know there were still challenges ahead after my first trip to Teotihuacán. Yes, challenges ahead for sure. But once I had experienced such a sweet taste of what it feels like to live fully in Heaven on Earth, and to know without a doubt that I could never be satisfied with anything less, there was no going back. At first, when I returned, I felt so energetically different than ever before. I was riding an emotional high for several weeks that nothing in my life could touch. Life was sweet and filled with magic that I could experience whenever I chose.

However, I was a wife and mother with a very stressful and challenging job at the university. Most of the people in my life expected me to be the same person I had been before. So, as don Miguel, Trey, and others had warned, it would be easy to fall back into old habits and ways of being in the world. I knew how to catch myself whenever I felt myself begin to slip. Around this time, my 23-year marriage was dissolving. For a while, it almost seemed like I was riding a roller coaster of emotional experience.

Practice makes the master, as don Miguel often said. I did practice. I kept attending our apprentice gatherings and met regularly with fellow apprentices who lived nearby. We continued to share our love and respect, and have many wonderful times together. Most importantly, I continued to pay attention to the words I used with myself and with others. I did my best to be impeccable with my word and not take anything personally. I listened to my inner judge and my inner victim, and gradually, they became less and less vocal. I paid attention to my emotional reactions and made a new choice when I didn't like the way something felt.

I did my best to choose love over fear each moment in my thoughts and actions. For several months during this time, I was noticing that it felt like my heart was expanding, both energetically and physically. I felt a physical pressure around my heart that seemed like there wasn't enough room in my chest anymore. Sometimes, it was even a little painful. I was pretty sure it wasn't anything to worry about at my age, but I was surprised to feel these physical sensations going on for months. One day, I said to don Miguel, "Miguel, my heart hurts!" His response was, "Don't worry, Sweetheart. Soon it's going to pop, like popcorn!" Well, that image was reassuring!

Many times each day, I would check in with myself to question whether or not I still believed something that I may have previously believed. My daily experiences often brought old beliefs and assumptions directly to my attention. It was easier and easier to see behind the curtain of belief that had once been unquestioned. Eventually, I began to experience what don Miguel had called the ghost phase. This was a very difficult time for me, in many ways. The ghost phase happens when you come to a place where nothing seems real anymore because you have questioned and released all of your old beliefs. In this phase, you no longer believe in anything. Nothing seemed important, either. That was the hardest part for me. I didn't feel depressed, exactly. I just felt like I was going through the motions at home or at work, but it was all meaningless. I just couldn't shake that feeling.

Of course, don Miguel told us how we could get out of the ghost phase. He would say that it's as if we were dragging our old corpse around. He wanted us to finally let go of that useless, heavy corpse. But, to get beyond that phase, he would say that we now had to choose what to believe. Our beliefs could no longer be dictated by the outside world; they must now be our personal choice. It had to be an act of personal power. This was very difficult for me. How could I choose to believe in something when nothing was real or important? For me, the ghost phase continued for a few years.

After months and months had turned into years, I came to a point where I finally asked myself, "Is there anything that I know for sure is real? Is there anything at all that I can truly believe is real?" The one thing that I could truthfully say I believed was real is Love. "Love is real. I know that my very essence is Love. I don't know what I am, but I am, and I love!" Suddenly, but completely seamlessly, everything changed. It wasn't until a few days or weeks had passed that I realized my ghost phase was completely gone. I had chosen the one thing I could truly believe in, without question. I was now in love with life again.

My life at that point improved tremendously, with an inner joy that permeates each moment. Do I sometimes forget to pay attention to this inner joy and get wrapped up in a momentary drama about relationships, work, politics, and the "outside dream"? Yes, I sometimes do. For the most part, I make an effort not to judge myself for making such a mistake, and I try to make a better choice as soon as possible. My emotions are an important key that I must pay close attention to. If I don't like how I'm feeling in a moment, I know that I need to change direction. When I realize that my attention has been diverted toward fear-based thoughts, I get to choose again.

I know now that suffering is a choice. Even physical pain or illness isn't as bad if I just let myself feel what I feel and do what I can to take care of my body. I understand that my resistance and my "story" can really make me suffer when I say, "Why do I feel so bad? Poor me. I shouldn't have to feel this way. What if I can't do my job? What if…what if…?" When I do that, it hurts much more. I have found that it is so much easier to just accept what is happening with as little resistance as possible. Then, take action to deal with it as best I can.

Another time in Teotihuacán comes to mind. Our group meeting was about to begin when I had to get up and rush out of the biblioteca in time to reach the women's restroom before being assaulted by a form of "Montezuma's Revenge." In my rush, I met don Miguel in the hallway. He asked, "Where are you going?" When I responded, he said, "Enjoy it, Sweetheart!" For me, that was a whole new way to experience this occasion!

Even animals, don Miguel would say, "Don't really suffer; they just feel the pain without any story. It's the story that makes us suffer." One time during my apprenticeship, I was sad because my dog, Sachi, had cancer in her jaw. When don Miguel asked me what was wrong, I told him. His response was that I should get a new dog. Well, I wasn't ready to give up on Sachi yet. So, after the surgery that removed her lower jaw back to her molars, I observed her closely. She obviously was in pain at first, but she seemed to handle it well. I hand-fed her until she could eat by herself. Eventually, she was able to fetch her ball and live as happily as ever.

In contrast, I knew that I, and most humans, would be saying things like; "This is awful. Why is this happening to me? How can I ever go out in public without a lower jaw and my tongue hanging down?" Sachi never cared when children exclaimed, "That dog has a really long tongue!"

There were many experiences over the years of my apprenticeship that have helped me to understand how I can learn to experience life in wonderful ways. Many years ago, my friend Silver told me about an experience she had while visiting Gini's ranch near Santa Fe, New Mexico, for a "Mini Teo" celebration. Silver was sitting on a fence outside during a break when don Miguel came up to her. She expressed to him how much she was enjoying the beauty around her. In an act of love and service, he told her, "I am going to lend you my eyes for the next 20 minutes. When I look around me, everything I see reflects love. I send my love to my surroundings, and that love is reflected back to me through my eyes. I want you to see the world the way I see the world."

Silver told me how beautiful and sweet her experience of the world became during those minutes when she saw it through don Miguel's "eyes". She said that everything seemed to sparkle and shine with beauty and love. I listened admiringly to her story, and I remember thinking to myself that this was how the world should appear. Why not? I certainly wanted to see the world that way. In that moment, I made a decision to "go for it!"

During another Teotihuacán journey, I was in the hotel dining room with my friend Gae, when don Miguel came up to us and gave her an assignment to "make love to the wall" next to her chair. I remember looking up at the wall. It was a plain, fairly smooth yet unimpressive, off-white, painted plaster wall that reached up to the high ceiling. Gae kind of looked at the wall, then at me, then at don Miguel as he turned to walk away. She decided to try and give it a go. It was hard for me to tell whether she was actually "getting into it" or even enjoying making love to the wall, but I decided to give her some space for her lovemaking experience. At the time, I wondered how well I could achieve making love to that wall. Today, I understand that everything around me reflects love when the love is coming out of me.

Ever since the day when I chose to believe in love, everything I see in the world around me reflects love back to me. Everything has a beautiful radiance that I can easily get lost in wherever and whenever I stop for a second to enjoy its radiance. I see it in a tree, feel it in the wind, taste it in a sip of tea. I feel it in the air I breathe. Such beauty is everywhere! Everything is alive and radiating. Actually, it may be that the light between me and everything around me is the thing that is most alive.

One of my most profound moments of realization happened about a year after I returned from my first trip to Teotihuacán. I was on my knees in my bathroom on a cold winter day, scraping old grout from around the basin of our shower stall. While this may never before have seemed like a fun or even comfortable job, I realized that I was completely in heaven at that moment! The beauty of being alive and appreciating my body, the light around me, and the simple joy of this moment brought tears to my eyes. I thought of the swami in India who exclaimed, "I never allow anyone to cook or clean for me. They think it's work. When I cook, even the rice sings bhajans!"

My apprenticeship and the many experiences and journeys over the years with don Miguel and my fellow travelers have brought me to a place of joyful gratitude for life and for the many blessings I continue to receive from them. Now, I finally understand that I am not made of matter. I am not made of stars. I am made of the living light between the stars! I am alive here in a human body, directing my attention each moment in thousands of new ways to the dance of light within and around me.

"To suffer is just a choice.

To be happy and to live

In a divine romance with life

Is also a choice."

- don Miguel Ruiz

About The Author

Christine Judal has always been inspired by service. This inspiration has guided her through a variety of life experiences. During her decade as a teacher, she instilled a love for learning in her students, fostering critical thinking, self-esteem, and creativity. Transitioning into federal civilian service, Christine developed technical expertise as an Air Force Quality Assurance Specialist, ensuring aircraft components met rigorous standards. Her passion for safety led her to become an Environmental Health and Safety Specialist for the University of California, where she championed workplace safety and environmental protection until her retirement. When she was offered the unique opportunity to apprentice under don Miguel Ruiz, author of The Four Agreements, she was grateful to deepen her spiritual and personal growth. From don Miguel, she learned the value of changing our early agreements with life when they no longer serve our truth. As an author, Christine hopes to pass on this legacy, serving with commitment to shine a light for others to find their own way home.